ᴀʏ Lɪꜰᴇ ᴡɪᴛʜ Gᴇᴏʀɢᴇ

MY LIFE WITH GEORGE

WHAT I LEARNED ABOUT JOY FROM ONE NEUROTIC (AND VERY EXPENSIVE) DOG

JUDITH SUMMERS

**WHEELER
WINDSOR
PARAGON**

This Large Print edition is published by Wheeler Publishing, Waterville, Maine, USA and by BBC Audiobooks Ltd, Bath, England.

Wheeler Publishing, a part of Gale, Cengage Learning.

The text of this Large Print edition is unabridged.

Other aspects of the book may vary from the original edition.

Set in 16 pt. Plantin.

Printed on permanent paper.

LIBRARY OF CONGRESS CATALOGING-IN-PUBLICATION DATA

Summers, Judith.
  My life with George : what I learned about joy from one neurotic (and very expensive) dog / by Judith Summers. — Large print ed.
      p. cm.
  Originally published: New York : Voice/Hyperion, 2007.
  ISBN-13: 978-1-59722-711-7 (hardcover : alk. paper)
  ISBN-10: 1-59722-711-0 (hardcover : alk. paper)
  1. Cavalier King Charles spaniel — England — London — Anecdotes. 2. Summers, Judith. 3. Women dog owners — England — London — Anecdotes. 4. Human-animal relationships — Anecdotes. I. Title.
SF429.C36S86 2007b
636.752'4—dc22   2007046597

BRITISH LIBRARY CATALOGUING-IN-PUBLICATION DATA AVAILABLE

Published in 2008 in the U.S. by arrangement with Voice, an imprint of Hyperion, a division of Buena Vista Books, Inc.

Published in 2008 in the U.K. by arrangement with The Penguin Group Limited.

U.K. Hardcover: 978 1 405 68672 3 (Windsor Large Print)
U.K. Softcover: 978 1 405 68673 0 (Paragon Large Print)

Printed in the United States of America
1 2 3 4 5 6 7 12 11 10 09 08

In loving memory of David Summers
and Udi Eichler

ACKNOWLEDGMENTS

This is a true story. To safeguard the privacy of the people who appear in it I have changed some of their names and disguised some identities.

My family and friends have been a constant source of emotional support over the last nine years. Now some of them have found themselves on the page. *No good deed goes unpunished,* as my father would have said. I am very grateful to all of them for allowing me to write about them.

I'd like to thank my agent, Clare Alexander, who was a moving force behind this book from its conception; Katy Follain at Penguin/Michael Joseph in London; and Ellen Archer and Pamela Dorman at Voice/Hyperion, New York.

My Life with George started as a newspaper article. It took my brother-in-law, Philip Norman, to suggest that I turn it into a book, and I can't thank him enough for the idea.

Very special thanks — in the shape of roast chicken — to the eponymous George, who provided me with constant inspiration and selflessly slept through the writing of this book.

And, most important, I owe a huge debt of thanks to my son, Joshua, for courageously allowing me to set down our lives on paper.

Judith Summers, May 2007

PROLOGUE

The alarm wakes me up at six thirty prompt.
Not the clock on my bedside table, which is
set for seven fifteen, but a piercing bark
from down the hall.

I pull a pillow over my head and try to get
back to sleep. There's a fat chance of that,
because the bark alarm has no off button. It
repeats at thirty-second intervals until I feel
thoroughly guilty. After all, it's been shut up
inside the house since midnight, and is
probably desperate for a pee.

I roll out of bed, stagger down the hall,
and open the study door. Eleven and a half
kilos of Cavalier King Charles Spaniel is lying at the ready beside his basket, hindquarters splayed out behind him, tail swishing
the floor like a starter's flag. In a split
second he's up and running, pushing between my legs without so much as a cursory
glance at me. And instead of heading for
the cat flap that leads into the garden, he

runs upstairs toward the kitchen, still barking, with a victorious glint in his eyes.

George might be bursting for a pee, but what he wants even more urgently is his breakfast.

Furious with myself for having been taken in by the same stunt George pulled yesterday, and the day before, and the day before that, I head back to bed. But a minute later, a wet black nose appears beside my pillow, along with a pair of feathery white paws and a cloud of warm dog breath. "Go away!" I murmur, only rather less politely. Not one to give up easily, George keeps up a persistent one-sided conversation at my bedside. There's only one way to get rid of him at this time in the morning, and that's to give in.

Upstairs in the open-plan kitchen-cum-living-room, he throws himself down as close to the refrigerator as he can get without blocking its door and stares at me with an unflinching gaze. I dole a generous portion of all-in-one dry dog food into his bowl and put it down on the slate hearthstone, but instead of jumping up to eat it, George doesn't budge an inch. He knows what's in there — a rubble of round, brown biscuits — and they tempt him far less than the identical-looking rabbit droppings that litter Hampstead Heath. Loaded with meaning, his eyes roll toward the fridge door, then back to me. What George wants is sitting inside that humming metal box. And just to make sure that I've got the message, he repeats the eye rolling a couple of times and licks his lips.

For an animal whose brain is the size and consistency of a mushroom, George has pretty effective communication skills.

Relenting — after all, I wouldn't want to eat those rabbit droppings either — I open the fridge door and take out the carcass of last night's roast chicken. George dances a salsa of anticipation around my feet as I tear off a few morsels and add them to his bowl, and when I carry it to the hearthstone, he skids backward in front of me, unwilling to take his eyes off it for an instant. Even before it has hit the floor, he's dived into it. By the time I've turned around, he's picked out every sliver of chicken and is already barking for more.

"Sorry, kiddo," I say firmly, "that's your lot." George is definitely on the chunky side. He's been on a weight-loss diet ever since he recovered from anorexia, and I'm supposed to see that he sticks to it.

He returns to the fridge and barks intermittently at its closed door. Doing my best to ignore him, I make a stab at clearing up the trail of detritus left lying around late last night by my seventeen-year-old son: the discarded sweater scrunched up between the sofa cushions, the mobile phone on the draining board, the poker chips on the mantelpiece, the open carton of milk souring on the coffee table, the three sneakers (why always three?) strewn treacherously across the rug, just where I'm most likely to trip over them. Eventually George stops barking, leaps up onto an armchair, and glares at me sulkily. Slowly but surely, his head droops. He's accepted that he's going to get nothing else to eat in the immediate future and settles down to his favorite leisure activity: deep, comatose sleep.

At eight fifteen, having roused my son from *his* comatose sleep and packed him off to school, I wake George. Since he knows what's next on the day's agenda, he raises his head with great reluctance and looks at me with dread. Intent on getting my own back for being woken so early myself, I cry "Walkies!" in my most enthusiastic tone, hook on his leash, drag him off the armchair, and pull him out of the front door. With a wistful backward glance at the house, George trots down the road beside me, wagging his tail at every parked car in the hope that we're going to get into it. Walkies in the car — that is, sitting upright in the front passenger seat and staring out at the passing scenery — is George's favorite form of exercise, which is why he has a weight problem.

I stride firmly past the cars, while my recalcitrant Cavalier lags further and further behind me on his extendable leash. This is just for starters. When he sees the Heath looming in front of him, he digs in his claws and grinds to a complete halt. I give the five meters of cord that now separates us a gentle jerk, but George doesn't budge. I try coaxing him, "Come on, darling!" but when he still doesn't move, exasperation breaks through: "Come ON! George! Heel! HEEL, I said! DO AS YOU'RE TOLD!"

George plants his large posterior four-square on the pavement. Like gangsters at a showdown, we glare at each other along the leash. I remember what the pet behaviorist I consulted told me: that I must show George who's top dog, and never let him get the better of me. "Okay," I say, as calmly as I can. "That's enough!" Turning away from him, I carry on walking, and since George refuses to stop his sit-down protest, he's dragged along behind me on his bottom. His collar works its way over one ear, and like the drama king that he is, he starts to cough and choke as if he's being strangled.

"Oh, look at that poor little doggie!"

A group of children on their way to the local primary school take pity on him, so I'm forced to stop. They surround George, crying, "Oh, he's so cute!" Fluttering his eyelashes, George jumps to his feet and snuggles up to them as if chocolate wouldn't melt in his mouth. But as their mothers approach, he moves to one side, arches his back, and . . .

"Yuck!"

George lands a perfect rosette on the pavement. As I bend down to scoop it into a hygienic plastic bag, the mothers catch up with their squealing offspring. They glare at George and at me with revulsion, as if I'm letting down the tone of the neighborhood. As fast as I can, I tie up the bag's handles to stop the smell escaping, but I'm not quick enough off the mark. Powdered nostrils flaring, the women give an involuntary shudder and pull their children away. One shoots me such a filthy look that you'd have thought that I'd made the mess myself.

As I stand there, humiliated, the plastic bag and its warm, squidgy contents dangling from my hand, I feel inexplicably annoyed with George. It's bad enough that I'm one of the few dog owners in posh Hampstead who actually walks her own dog, rather than employing a professional to do it, without having to pick up his feces, too. Besides, similar incidents to this one happen with such regularity that I'm beginning to suspect George engineers them on purpose in order to embarrass me in front of my own species. In other words, he's getting his own back for being taken on a walk against his wishes. Can this be true? Does my dog defecate at will out of a desire for revenge? Or am I barking mad?

Now comes the matter of bag disposal in the receptacle at the end of our street. There it stands, a mud-splattered, mailbox red contraption bristling with E. coli and toxocara germs. Holding my breath to stop myself gagging, I lift its lid with the very tip of one finger, drop in the bag, and run away before I'm overcome with toxic fumes. This, I remind myself, is the downside of dog owning.

Sometimes, at this hour of the day, it's hard to remember what the upside is.

George does a 180-degree turn in the direction of home — after all, he's done his business now and can't see what further purpose would be served by continuing the walk — but I'm having none of it. Tightening his leash, I pull him across the road that separates the residential streets of Hampstead village from the 791 open acres of our local park, the Heath. Then I congratulate myself on having scored a major victory: I've actually got George out here, and it's only eight forty-five. Realizing that it's useless to try to get out of the enforced march, he plods along behind me with a down-turned mouth. He may be going walkies, but he's damned if he's going to enjoy it.

I unleash George when we turn off the tree-lined path onto the large meadow that slopes down to the ponds at South End Green. All around us retrievers, Labradors, Alsatians, Dalmatians, dachshunds, Jack Russells, and assorted mutts are bounding through the long grass, running after balls, fetching sticks, or simply trotting happily beside their owners. Unlike them, my Cavalier stays rooted to the spot while I stride ahead. Halfway across the field, I glance surreptitiously over my shoulder to see if he's following me. No, he's still in exactly the same place as he was when I unleashed him. As usual, George is taking a stand against walking by standing still.

I call him to heel. I shout. I whistle. I yell. George remains as immobile as the cute stuffed toy he so resembles. Only when I dodge behind a tree and he can no longer see me does he come to life. Afraid of losing his meal ticket, he takes a few tentative steps in my direction and then breaks into a fast trot and, finally, a frantic run.

And as he runs, a wonderful transformation takes place: George's miserable expression dissolves. I could swear that he's smiling, perhaps even grinning. Even a dog as exercise-shy as he is can't resist a run on the Heath on a sunny spring morning when the air is brisk and fresh.

Suddenly George is a different animal. Or rather, he *is* an animal. Nose to the ground like the hunting dogs from which his breed is descended, he follows the scent of a thousand rabbits, squirrels, and foxes and runs hither and thither across the field. He puts up basking woodpeckers and charges at magpies. He chases squirrels up trees and laps water from muddy puddles. Stopping to sniff the earth, he falls onto his back and rolls sensuously from side to side, kicking his legs merrily in the air.

I sit down on a bench and watch him. My aggravation melts away. Okay, George is difficult, willful, and stubborn and doesn't like being in the open air. He doesn't chase balls like normal dogs. He doesn't obey commands, bring back sticks, shake paws, or do any other tricks. In fact, he's pretty useless. All he's good for is eating chicken, barking, tearing up tissues, and being waited on hand and foot. But every now and then he stops being a spoiled brat of a royal prince and reverts to being an ordinary mutt, full of pure, exuberant animal joy.

Well-satisfied by his long roll in the grass, and looking extraordinarily, smugly pleased with himself, George jumps to his feet, notes where I am, hurtles across the field toward me, and hurls himself onto my lap. Overcome with emotion for Woman's Best Friend, I give him a hug and kiss the white fluffy fur on top of his adorable head. "Good boy," I coo, like the dog-mad lady I am at heart. "I *do* love you, Georgie-Porgie!"

Then, as we sit on the bench together, a woman and her dog in happy harmony, a pungent, noxious smell rises from his warm body. I look down and discover that George hasn't been rolling on the ground simply for the pleasure of it. No, he's been rolling *in* something — and it's sticky, brown, and disgusting. Whatever it is — and I don't like to think about it in too much detail — it's all over his back, his muzzle, his hind legs, and his front paws. Not only is *he* covered in it, so am I.

I push the monster off my lap and wipe my dirty, sticky hands on a clump of grass. I attach the leash to his collar and head for home. George leads the way, his tail hoisted high and waving like a tattered flag of victory. As well it might. Against all expectation he has turned the tables on me and won the battle: our morning walk, which I had planned to last at least forty minutes, is over after just ten.

The moment I'm through the front door, I tear off my filthy clothes and throw George into the bath, but not before he's rolled on the hall carpet and smeared it with the substance he's covered with. I wash and shampoo him, then dry him with my hairdryer. I shampoo the hall carpet, and then scour the bath. Finally I scrub myself, put on some clean clothes, and throw my jeans into the washing machine with George's dirty towels.

I then stuff my stained coat into a plastic bag and take it to the dry cleaner in the village. This time when I leave the house, George stays behind. As I walk down the garden path, he leaps onto the back of the sofa and looks at me reproachfully through the bay window. Why are you abandoning me? he seems to say.

19

I return home to find him lying on my white duvet cover, which has, in the last half hour, mysteriously acquired a *101 Dalmatians* theme and is covered in big gray paw prints. He's fast asleep and snoring, with his wrinkled little nose resting between his giant paws. Even though officially he's not allowed on the bed, he looks so peaceful that I can't bring myself to disturb him. Instead of starting work, I throw myself down beside him.

It's only ten thirty, but I'm exhausted. I've been up for four hours, and in one way or another, George has dominated all of them.

Why, oh, why, I ask myself, did I ever get a dog?

ONE

It was 1998, and the first week of November. The clocks had recently been turned back, marking the official start of winter, and as I walked my nine-year-old son, Joshua, home from school, the darkness was drawing in.

In past years, we'd returned home on afternoons just like this one to find all the lights blazing. As we'd come through the front door, we'd hear loud jazz or flamenco music coming from the CD player, usually mixed with the highbrow tones of a Radio 4 chat show, and often the soundtrack of a video playing on the TV. A deeply animated, and occasionally infuriated, male voice rose above the cacophony. Udi Eichler, my husband and Joshua's father, was seated in his favorite chair at the end of the kitchen table, talking on the telephone.

Invariably Udi was surrounded by a sea of newspapers, political and literary journals, magazines on speedboating, half-read Booker Prize contenders, cups of cold black coffee, unanswered letters, scrawled-upon notepads, topless pens, and open blue plastic pouches of Gauloises tobacco. Oh, yes, and his beloved Psion Organizer, a machine from which he was never willingly parted. Often he was juggling two telephone calls at once — one on our landline, the other on his mobile, which was tucked uncomfortably between shoulder and ear. Stuck between the fingers of his right hand, the thin, moist roll-up looked more like a badly rolled joint than the ordinary cigarette it actually was. As Udi puffed steadily on it, dripping ash everywhere except into the pristine ashtray in front of him, wisps of smoke rose slowly into the air and settled in a ghostly halo above his head.

This year, as Joshua and I walked down our street, I had a leaden feeling inside me. Our house was dark and silent. There wasn't a single light on in the kitchen, and there was no John Coltrane or Gypsy Kings music seeping through the sash windows. I chatted brightly to Joshua as we came up the path, hoping he wouldn't notice how different things were from how they'd once been, but I don't think he was fooled for a minute.

"How were sports today, darling?"

"It's not *sports,* it's *football.* And it was rained out."

"Oh. What a pity! What did you do instead?"

"Nothing."

"Oh. Nothing at all? Didn't Miss Sandra suggest anything?"

"She was busy. We mucked around in the classroom."

"That must have been fun. So, have you got much homework tonight?"

"Just some maths. Why are you asking all these questions?"

"Because I'm interested."

"Why? It's school, Mum. And you ask the same things every day."

I turned my key in the front door, but with no pleasure. There were few things I disliked more than coming home to an empty house. With Udi around, our home had been full to the point of overflowing. Now, instead of the tornado of activity he'd generated around him, there was an uncanny stillness inside the rooms. Rambling on to Joshua about what I'd done that day, I quickly turned on all the lights, closed the wooden shutters over the blackening windows, and lit the gas log fire in the grate. I tuned the radio to a rock music station and, for good measure, switched on the television. The purpose of all this was to disguise Udi's tangible absence — symbolized by the empty Carver chair at the end of the bare kitchen table, which had once been his throne.

Udi had died five months before, at the age of fifty-six. He'd steamrollered into my life thirteen years earlier, wearing a fur-trimmed coat he'd bought in an Oxfam shop and a black fedora given to him by the American writer Saul Bellow. An extrovert Mitteleuropean who overflowed with joie de vivre, he was a renowned maker of TV documentaries; and he was also training to become a psychotherapist. Brilliant, charismatic, provocative, and with the gift of the gab, Udi had interests that ranged from art through to windsurfing, and he could hold forth for hours on any subject from outboard motors to postmodernist literature. If there was one adjective you could never have used to describe him, it was boring.

Udi had the knack of dominating any space he occupied, be it an office, a kitchen, or a dinner party, an arena in which he delighted in prodding — or rather exploding — his fellow guests out of any complacent views they might hold. Far from being an intellectual snob, he treated everyone with the same respect: from writers such as

Bellow, whom he had met through his work as a TV producer, to Joseph, the Ethiopian mini-cab driver he had befriended. Udi spent hours, sometimes months, helping acquaintances and friends sort out their personal problems. He was genuinely fascinated by everyone with whom he came into contact.

Perhaps he was so generous with himself and lived life with such gusto because his own childhood had been hard. He'd been born with a clubfoot in 1942 in Nazi-occupied Austria, to a narcissistic seventeen-year-old mother, Gertie, who then worked her way through six husbands in almost as many years. As for Udi's real father, he had little to do with him.

When Udi was a troubled thirteen-year-old, Gertie sent him to England for a fortnight's holiday with Gus, the owner of a Bohemian restaurant-cum-jazz-club off London's Fulham Road and the only one of her ex-husbands who took any interest in her son. To Gus's horror, at the end of two weeks Udi announced his intention of remaining in England for good, and refused to go home. When Gus turned him out with a five-pound note in his pocket, Udi threw himself on the mercy of the Home Office. He felt British, not Austrian, he told the powers that be, and he wanted to stay here forever.

The Home Office of the mid-1950s was a very different place from the strictly regulated, bureaucracy-laden organization it is today. Bewildered, and perhaps amused, by the thirteen-year-old Austrian's determination, its civil servants not only granted him leave to stay but took him into care. After packing him off to a young offenders' institution for six months — they simply didn't know what else to do with him — they found him a place at the Inner London Education Authority's only state-run boarding school, a marvelous institution near Ipswich called Woolverstone Hall. From there, he went on to study economics at university, and then joined the staff of BBC Television under their graduate general-trainee scheme.

Initially Udi hadn't been my parents' choice as a perfect partner for their precious younger daughter. The thing was, they'd never met anyone like him — few people had — and they didn't know what to make of him. Recently separated from Diana, his wife of twenty-four years, Udi was eleven years older than I was. Having married at the age of nineteen, he already had two grown-up daughters, Tabby and

Hannah, who'd been brought up in a unique, psychotherapeutically based community in Kew, West London. Udi drove around on an old motorbike wearing a battered crash helmet, a floral shirt, and skintight black leather trousers my father disparagingly called his lederhosen. His shoes were leprechaun green. He chain-smoked roll-ups, and dropped ash everywhere, distributing it across carpets, tabletops, and clothes as if he were performing some sort of benediction rite. His conversation ranged from Nietzsche and libertarianism to the most intimate questions (a typical opening gambit to a perfect stranger might be "Tell me about your first sexual experience," and the odd thing was that the stranger usually did). Questions such as these might have gone down well among London's literati, but in conventional, Jewish middle-class society this kind of behavior was greeted with suspicion, not to say scandalized shock.

I was in my thirties, however, and still unmarried, so my parents accepted Udi. And from the moment their first grandchild, Joshua, was born, Udi could do little wrong in their eyes. In time they grew to love my oddball and outstandingly hospitable husband dearly, and he them.

Although he was overweight, smoked like

a chimney, and ran on endless liters of strong black coffee, Udi always seemed to enjoy good health, so my constant warnings to him about obesity, heart attacks, and lung cancer fell on deaf ears. But by May 1997 he was looking and feeling awful. His skin had a gray cast, he was troubled by pains in his chest, which he insisted were caused by indigestion, and he'd often come home from work and fall asleep on the sofa. This was highly unusual behavior for a human dynamo who ordinarily didn't go to bed until three in the morning, then woke up four hours later, refreshed and ready to go.

It took much nagging on my part to get him to see a doctor. As a trained psychotherapist and a physician manqué, Udi would spend ages diagnosing other people's medical or psychological problems, yet he somehow felt he was above needing help himself. But in early June he suddenly found it difficult to swallow, and the trip to the doctor could no longer be postponed.

She referred Udi for an endoscopy at our local hospital, the Royal Free in Hampstead. Since he had a business meeting to go to immediately afterward, he insisted on undergoing the throat examination without an anesthetic, or even a sedative. He emerged from the experience nauseated and shaken.

Something was clearly wrong with him, and he feared it was serious.

A few minutes later the consultant summoned us into his office, where he greeted us with the chilling words "I'm so very sorry." Udi, he said, had cancer of the esophagus, and the prognosis was not good. In the short term he'd have a dangerous operation to remove a large section of his throat, but even so, the chances of his making a full recovery were slim.

As it happened, the diagnosis — but, tragically, not the prognosis — was wrong. The small tumor that the specialist had spotted at the base of Udi's esophagus was but the tip of an iceberg: a huge tumor had been growing inside the lining of his stomach for an indeterminate number of years. By the time it was detected, it had broken through the stomach walls and had reached the size of a house brick. As Professor Marc Winslett, Udi's brilliant surgeon, deduced from his subsequent MRI scans, Udi was suffering from stage IV *linitis plastica,* a rare form of gastric cancer. The outlook could hardly have been worse.

At the end of August, in a life-threatening, six-hour operation, Winslett removed the huge malignant growth, along with Udi's entire stomach. He then created a tiny new false "stomach" out of a short length of Udi's intestine. From now on, like a crash dieter who'd had his stomach stapled, Udi would only be able to eat small amounts at a time, and his weight would drop dramatically. "You always wanted a slim husband," he quipped from the hospital bed as he was wheeled into the operating theater. "Now you'll have one."

Never an easy patient, my libertarian husband started to play up the moment he regained consciousness in Intensive Care by demanding that, in the name of personal freedom, he be allowed a cigarette. In vain did the nurses protest that (a) a roll-up was the last thing he needed, (b) the hospital was a smoke-free zone, (c) the smoke might kill his fellow patients in the unit, and (d) lighting up while a supply of pure oxygen was being fed into his nostrils might cause Udi to explode. Though barely compos mentis after his long anesthetic, and hooked up to countless monitors and drips, he nagged and nagged until, twelve hours later, the IC staff could stand it no longer and shipped him back to the gastrointestinal ward a full day before they were supposed to.

A few nights later, just after I'd left his bedside, Udi walked out of the ward on impulse, undetected by the nurses. Ebullient at having survived his surgery, he was determined not to waste a single hour of whatever future remained to him in staring at grim hospital walls. Held together from sternum to navel by a line of metal staples, and wearing only his pajamas and dressing gown, he bummed a lift up the hill from one of the other patients' visitors and arrived home, without his keys, to find no one in. Taking a chance that Joshua and I were at my sister's house around the corner (we were), he walked there in his bare feet and surprised us all. A glass of orange juice in his hand, one leg crossed nonchalantly over the other, surrounded by the family, he laughed and joked as if he was on top of the world. He seemed invincible.

Yet ten months later he was dead. What his oncologist described as "an aggressive regime" of chemotherapy — administered, the specialist admitted, with the proviso that he hadn't a clue whether it would work — had neither given Udi the miracle cure he had hoped for nor bought him the two to three extra years of life that had been the least of his expectations. In fact, it had done nothing more than make him feel dreadfully ill, and temporarily hold back the tide of minute cancer cells that had already metastasized throughout his body.

Invisible, undetectable, yet as lethal as the spores of some poisonous fungus, they sat inside him waiting for an opportunity to sprout into life — and they did so the moment that the three-month course of chemotherapy ended. In January, when he took the whole family on a skiing holiday to Austria, Udi seemed almost back to normal. But he wasn't. By late March, when he underwent an emergency operation to remove a small blockage in his intestines, we were told that his life expectancy was no more than six months. By early May, after a third operation, this all-too-short time scale had shrunk to a minuscule three weeks.

A three-week death sentence was not only deeply shocking but virtually impossible to take on board, particularly since Udi still seemed as much of a live wire as ever. Fired up on a self-administered morphine drip, which was delivered to him at home by a team of palliative-care nurses he nicknamed the "Death Squad," he continued to go out for coffee with his friends until he was too weak to do so. From then on he held court on the living room sofa, and later in a hospice, where a steady stream of friends, family, and acquaintances came to bid him farewell. So many arrived — some from as far afield as America — that, like the PA of a busy government minister, I had to keep a diary of their visits and limit the length of time they stayed so that they didn't all swamp us at once.

To be frank, making thirty cups of coffee a day and handing out comfort and tissues to a stream of distraught people as they left our house in floods of tears was not the ideal way to spend the last days with my husband — and, to make matters worse, my father, who lived in France, was dying of cancer at exactly the same time and I couldn't get away to visit him. But this was Udi's death, not mine, and he had the right to conduct it in whichever way he saw fit, so I bit my lip. Others saw his constant socializing and blunt, stoical attitude to his imminent death as heroic, almost saintly. I interpreted it otherwise. Terrified of dying, Udi was avoiding being alone with those to whom he was closest: me, who had been his partner and wife for the last thirteen years; Tabby and Hannah, his much-loved grown-up daughters, who moved in with us during the final weeks to help care for him; Nathaniel, his adorable four-year-old grandson; and, most of all, eight-year-old Joshua, who sat on the hospice bed, painting his father's toenails bright pink. Udi proudly showed them to all his visitors and laughed, but the laughter held a bitter ring. He adored Joshua, and the thought that he would not live to see him grow up was unbearably painful to him.

Joshua had known from the start that something was seriously wrong with his father. The huge operation, which had left him with a scar reminiscent of Dr. Frankenstein's monster down his stomach, could hardly have been kept secret. Neither could the months of chemotherapy that had sapped Udi's strength, made him bad-tempered and tired, and caused his hair to fall out. Besides, as a psychotherapist Udi didn't believe in keeping secrets from anyone, even children. It was always better to face the truth, he insisted, even when it was painful to hear.

"Is Dad going to get better?" was a question Joshua had often asked me in the beginning.

"I certainly hope so!" I'd answered, in the kind of indignant voice that made it sound like a given. It wasn't a lie. Despite the terrible odds, I'd honestly believed that Udi would survive. He'd always been a lucky so-and-so who sailed close to the wind in his personal relationships as well as professionally. He courted danger, yet somehow always managed to avoid it at the last minute.

Not this time, though.

As the months went past, despite my best efforts to keep up a cheerful and superficially normal home front, Joshua's face had begun to look as washed-out as his father's, and the question he'd asked me most frequently changed to "Is Dad going to die?"

"I hope not," I'd replied at first, and later, "I don't think so." Joshua had made me promise not to lie to him: if Udi was going to die, he wanted to be told about it before it happened. So when I could avoid it no longer, my answer to his most FAQ had become "There's a chance that he will"; and then, "Yes, he might."

When Joshua countered innocently one day, "If he does, will I get the day off school?" I realized how little he understood of the enormity of what was about to happen, and what impact it would have on his life.

After Udi received his three weeks' notice from Professor Winslett, I had to become more blunt with Joshua. I knew that Udi would talk openly about his imminent death, both to visiting friends and on the telephone. If we didn't tell Joshua, he was bound to listen in to one of these conversations, which might be even worse than hearing the news from us directly.

So in the end we decided to tell him that, yes, Udi was probably going to die, and quite soon. It was a decision I immediately regretted. What was death in the mind of an eight-year-old? The thought that his father might do it — whatever *it* was — at any moment terrified him. He became nervous in Udi's company and only gradually relaxed again so that, by the end of the three weeks, he was designing a pyramid-shaped tomb for Udi and nursing him alongside his sister Hannah. "I'm so proud of you, Dad," I remember him saying as he tended Udi on the last day of his life.

Outwardly calm and resigned to death, inwardly raging at being deprived of his future and suffering the ignominy of his body's final breakdown, Udi died at dawn on the 3rd of June 1998. "So damn much not yet lived," he'd written to Professor Winslett a few weeks before. "Even though I have packed at least two lives into my time, it just hasn't been enough!" His cremation a week later, attended by more than two hundred and fifty people, was a secular celebration of his charismatic personality and his exceptional gifts for understanding and friendship. Unique, heroic, altruistic, challenging, exotic, an enabler of others, unquenchably inquisitive, loyal, idiosyncratic, inspiring, unflinchingly honest, vibrant, engaged, earthy, irreplaceable: these were just some of the words used to describe him. There were speeches by old friends and erstwhile television colleagues. His favorite aria from Mozart's *The Magic Flute* — "Dies Bildnif" — was sung by Robert Johnston, a young tenor who'd grown up in the Kew community where Udi had once lived. The actor John Thaw, one of Udi's many well-known psychotherapy clients, recited the Primo Levi poem "To My Friends." Tabby and Hannah read a very poignant tribute to their father, and Joshua recited a poem he'd written comparing Udi to a leaf blown away in a storm. He reduced everyone to tears.

My choice of final music for the service was Irving Berlin's 1930s classic "Cheek to Cheek." It had always been "our" song, though Udi could never remember any of the lyrics except one line — the first. Sung by Fred Astaire, it echoed around the red-brick crematorium as we all filed out. He was in heaven, the lyric went — and everybody burst out laughing.

I couldn't help thinking that if Udi had been there to act as host, the event would have been transformed into the most marvelous party. He'd have enjoyed the attention and flattering comments immensely. And, a TV producer to the core, he would almost certainly have suggested several changes to the running order.

The following day my sister, Sue, and I took our children to France to visit our desperately ill seventy-nine-year-old father, David, whom I hadn't seen for months. He'd been very sick but still on his feet when I'd last visited him. Now he was too weak to stand, or even open his eyes.

When I'd been a small child, my father had seemed like the strongest man in the universe. He'd clench the muscles of his right arm and invite my sister and me to swing from it, crack a walnut between his fingers or break an apple in two with his bare hands, just to impress us. Behind his physical strength had lain a soft heart, a gentlemanly character, and a generous nature. A greengrocer's son from the East End of London, he'd worked his way out of poverty when still relatively young, educated himself, and given us, his family, everything he'd lacked as a child. I was his younger daughter, and he'd spoiled me terribly.

During the last few months, my father and Udi had often joked over the telephone that they'd beat each other to the finishing line, but in the end Udi had won. Over the years my father had confided in Udi a way he never had in anyone else. He'd been heart-broken to learn of Udi's death, and deeply worried about my future and Joshua's. I sat beside his bed, held his hand, and tried to reassure him that we'd be all right.

As if he'd been waiting to say good-bye to his daughters and grandchildren, my father died less than twenty-four hours after we arrived in France. Understandably, Joshua was frightened by this second death, which came just eleven days after his father's. "All the men in our family are dying," he said in despair. He worried that he would be next.

We flew my father's body to England and, a day later, found ourselves at the cremato-rium in Golders Green for the second fam-ily funeral within a fortnight. Many of the same friends and relatives were there, too, so it felt rather like an instant replay of Udi's.

By some cruel irony, the shop windows everywhere that week were filled with Fa-ther's Day banners, gifts, and cards. I did my best to keep Joshua away from them, and not to look at them myself, but they were impossible to avoid. Every time I saw them it was like having salt rubbed into my two open wounds. I was distraught. In the privacy of our bedroom, I opened Udi's wardrobe and gazed blankly at the neatly arranged shirts and trousers that had suddenly become limp, useless relics. I slipped my hands inside shoes that still bore the imprint of Udi's feet, and buried my face in jackets he would never wear again. They smelled of his heat, of tobacco, of him.

Two

Following the two family funerals, I muddled though July and August in the same way as I'd muddled through the previous year, supported by a network of family and friends. Like my mother, my two aunts, my grandmother, and my great-aunt, I was now a widow — a ghastly word that still brings to mind lonely old ladies sitting in rocking chairs and knitting sweaters (I don't know why, because none of them was remotely like that). But, in my mid-forties, I certainly didn't want to be a member of the unenviable sisterhood of widows.

Joshua and I weren't alone in having lost people we loved. Tabby and Hannah had lost their father. My mother had lost her husband and her colorful, eccentric son-in-law. My niece Jessica had lost her grandfather, and my sister, Sue, had lost her father as well as the brother-in-law who'd been her friend and intellectual sparring partner. Though Sue was incredibly supportive of us, no one gave *her* much sympathy — they were too busy giving it to my mother, Joshua, and me.

As with all bereavements, no amount of forethought equipped us for the grief. You just have to work your way through it day by day. And when the person who has died was your soul mate and closest friend, perhaps the worst aspect of the experience is that the one you'd most like to talk to about what you're going through isn't around to discuss things. He's not even at the end of a telephone. He's completely vanished, just when you need him most. Outwardly I seemed cool, calm, and unnaturally collected. Inside I was overwhelmed and panicking, like a passenger on a rudderless ship from which the captain had fallen overboard. In denial, I filled the long summer days with activities and immediately threw myself back into life with as much enthusiasm as I could muster. I didn't want anyone pitying me or thinking I couldn't cope. At Joshua's school sports day, less than a week after Udi's death, I slapped on a smile, kicked off my shoes, rolled up my trousers, and competed in the parents' sack race, determined to show that, not only wasn't I miserable, I was as good as any of the fathers who were taking part. I was doing brilliantly until just before the finishing line when I turned my ankle and keeled over. To Joshua's embarrassment, I limped in last.

Since my mother still lived abroad, we went to France that August to spend a fortnight with her. I was preoccupied with Joshua the whole time. In previous years, he'd had his grandfather and his father to play with in the swimming pool. Now he was surrounded by a fussy, all-female posse consisting of his grandmother, his aunt, his younger cousin Jessica, and me. When he confided in me tearfully that Udi had promised to let him try a terrifying-looking and expensive sport in which you don a parachute and are towed in the air behind a speedboat, which Joshua was far too young to do alone, I was determined that he shouldn't miss out on the experience. Despite my twin fears of heights and water-skiing, I was soon strapped into a harness, attached to a parachute, and dangling high above the sea, with Joshua dangling next to me. I was so scared that I can hardly remember it — but I think I spent the whole time shouting, "Be careful!" in Joshua's left ear.

"I've got something to tell you, Mum," an exhilarated but sheepishly grinning Joshua said, when we were back on dry land. "Dad never promised to take me up in a parachute. I just wanted to do it."

Far from being angry, I regarded this blatant emotional manipulation as a sign that my son was doing better than I was. But, of course, losing his father was unavoidably and acutely painful. When we returned to London, Joshua often broke down in tears, unable to accept that the doctors hadn't been able to cure Udi. Other people had heart and lung transplants, so why couldn't he have had a tummy transplant? At other times Joshua lay on my bedroom floor, throwing a fit that other children still had their fathers and he did not. Why had *he* been singled out to suffer? I had no easy answers, and precious little comfort to offer him. All I could say was that this period of our lives would be an awful struggle — but, I promised him, we'd get through it somehow.

Before September was out Joshua had cut the words "Udi" and "Dad" from his vocabulary. Worried that he was becoming disassociated from what had happened (you can't live with a therapist for years without some of the psychobabble rubbing off on you) and inspired by a book I'd read on dealing with bereaved children, I chose one of Udi's photographs, took it down from the mantelpiece, and attempted to talk to Joshua about him. "Isn't this a lovely picture of Daddy?" I started, in a soothing voice.

Before I could say another word, my son froze me with a cold look and said, "You're trying to get me to talk about it, aren't you, Mum?"

I caught my breath. Was my son that clever, or was I that obvious? "No! Well . . . Yes, I suppose I am," I admitted, blushing like a thief who'd been caught with her fingers in the till. "But *I* want to talk about him, too, you know."

Joshua got up and walked out of the room with an emphatic "Well I don't!"

I'd been outsmarted by a child whose instinctive understanding of psychotherapy was obviously on a par with his father's and certainly far superior to mine. At that point I decided to let Joshua deal with his grief in his own way and in his own time, no matter what the experts said. I reassured him that I was there if ever he did want to talk about Udi, but I didn't push him any further.

I felt so sorry for Joshua, and so powerless to help him. At his age (he'd just turned nine) I knew he was too young to comprehend the finality of death. I could scarcely take it on board myself. He did know, however, that our lives had changed immeasurably, and very much for the worse. As a parent Udi, with his optimistic nature and daring, rather wild streak, had always been the one to say yes to any request or new idea, while I, despite my brief venture into parachuting, was by far the most cautious half of our duo and more likely to say no.

Now the person who'd generated the most activity, spontaneity, and fun in Joshua's life had ceased to exist, and he was stuck with me, his quieter, more anxious parent, rattling around in a home that seemed half-empty for the simple reason that it *was* half-empty. Udi's had been a big personality. Now that he wasn't around, the rooms sang with silence even when we were in them. The plumped-up pillows on his side of our king-size bed ached to be slept on. The kitchen table was no longer a mountain of clutter, there were no shirts to iron, and the telephone had virtually stopped ringing. A supermarket run, which had once been used up in a matter of days, now lasted us more than a week, and pushing a trolley around the aisles of Waitrose or Sainsbury's reduced me to tears every time. Since I couldn't bring myself to cook for just the two of us, and had lost my appetite completely, mounds of uneaten food rotted in our fridge.

The house felt even lonelier this time of year. The darkness outside the windows at five o'clock in the evening acted like a cold reality check. It seemed to accentuate that Joshua and I were holed up together, just the two of us, alone. As we sat opposite one another at the kitchen table eating chicken and French fries (I couldn't yet bring myself to sit in what I still regarded as Udi's chair at the head of the table), our knives and forks clanked against the crockery and I strained to keep up a conversation.

Suddenly, one night, he interrupted me with the fateful words "Mum, I think we should get a dog."

"A dog?" I was nonplussed. "What makes you say that?"

He speared a stick of potato with his fork and dunked it in tomato ketchup. "Tom has a dog. She's called Molly." Tom Alwyn was a new friend of Joshua's. He and his brother Joe, a year younger, had joined Joshua's school that September. Their parents, Elizabeth and Richard, were witty, warm, and enormously likeable, and Joshua had spent the previous Saturday afternoon playing at their child-friendly and wonderfully chaotic home.

"Tom and Joe have cats, too," Joshua went on. "Two. And guinea pigs that live in a cage under Tom's bed. They have lots of pets. There's always something going on in their house."

"It sounds like fun."

Joshua swallowed his French fry and looked across the table at me. "If you and me had a dog, well, we'd have someone to talk to when we came home."

"But we have each other to talk to!"

He looked away. "Someone *else* to talk to. Now that Dad's not here."

Joshua was wiser than I gave him credit for. Of course, he felt exactly as I did — that since Udi had died there had been a great emptiness in our lives that needed to be filled. But a dog was no substitute for a father or a husband. And the idea of the commitment it would involve horrified me. I'd had pets during my childhood, so I knew that dogs needed a lot of looking after. Five months after losing Udi and my father, I scarcely felt able to look after Joshua. In fact, I longed for some Mary Poppins figure to float through the front door with a tapestry bag hanging over her arm and take me in hand.

"I'll think about getting a dog," I said as noncommittally as I could.

Joshua's lower lip jutted out. "Huh! I suppose that means *no!*"

"It means I'll think about it."

My son put his head on one side and regarded me with a knowing look. Then he gave a long sigh and the corners of his mouth turned down. "Mum, remember what Dad always said?"

"What?"

His lips trembled as if he was about to cry. However, his eyes remained steadily fixed on mine, and I had a strange feeling that, as in the case of that parachute, I was about to be well and truly manipulated. I was right.

"He said, 'Always say *yes* when someone asks you if they can do something, unless there's a really, really good reason to say no to it.' Well, Mum, now that Dad's not here to say *yes* to things, don't you think *you* should say *yes* instead?"

THREE

On the following Saturday morning, Joshua and I were on our way to West London to visit the Kennel Club's annual Discover Dogs show at Earls Court.

Despite my reservations, I'd promised my son that I'd think seriously about getting a puppy. On the surface it wasn't a bad idea. As I'd grown up with pets myself, I knew just how important for a child a relationship with an animal could be. I'd also recently read a magazine article on something called pet-assisted therapy. Animals had been used to help people through troubled times apparently since the ninth century, when physically disabled people were given the job of looking after them in what is now the Belgian city of Geel. And when, in the eighteenth century, a Quaker tea merchant named William Tuke had opened the York Retreat, an enlightened asylum for the insane in the north of England, he'd used contact with animals to try to cure his patients. Since other treatments at the time included fettering lunatics to walls with iron chains, spinning them in special "whirling chairs" till blood poured out of their ears, plunging them into cold baths, and violent bloodletting, stroking an animal — even a wild one — could only have been an improvement.

In the words of that pioneer of modern nursing Florence Nightingale, who was bedridden for fourteen years in old age, a small pet was "often an excellent companion for the sick, for long chronic cases especially." Even the great Sigmund Freud had turned to his Chow for comfort during his terminal cancer. Siggie had known what he was doing, and nowadays animal-assisted therapy is all the rage. Playing with dogs and cats has been proven to lower blood pressure, aid recovery from strokes, and generally improve physical and mental health. Even non-furry mammals will do: a study by the University of Leicester found that swimming with dolphins helped patients to overcome depression.

But still, even though getting a puppy might be good for Joshua, I wasn't exactly enthusiastic about the idea. Being tied down by a dog was not on my immediate agenda.

In fact, it wasn't on any of my agendas. As we got off the tube at Earls Court, I tried hard not to think about the impracticality of it. We lived in a ground- and lower-ground-floor flat. With one open-plan room upstairs and our bedrooms downstairs, there was nowhere puddle-proof that we could keep a puppy until it was house-trained. At the least it would have the run of the ground floor, which meant there'd be puddles beside the sofa and on the living room rug, which might seep through the floorboards into the rooms below.

But what were a few stains and puddles compared to the joy and, I hoped, healing power that a puppy would bring to my distressed son? I asked myself as Joshua and I entered Discover Dogs. According to the promotional blurb, the show was the ideal place to learn more about the joys of canine companionship. It was a fun environment in which people could see dogs at their best. Unlike the exalted Crufts, where the pampered pooches were kept at a safe distance from the hoi polloi like celebrities at a movie premiere, Discover Dogs was definitely a "paws-on" experience. Not only could dog lovers buy an array of pet accessories that ranged from doggie Santa Claus hats to rhinestone leashes, they could discuss different breeds' faults and foibles with their owners, and even cuddle and stroke them — the dogs, not the humans. Though you couldn't actually buy dogs at the show — phew! — a hundred and eighty breeds would be on display so we'd have ample opportunity to choose the perfect canine companion to fit in with our lifestyle. Discover Dogs was definitely the try-before-you-buy event of the pet calendar.

Joshua and I trudged up and down the crowded aisles, visiting every stand, from those graced with elegant Afghan hounds to those stocked with hungry-looking Canadian huskies. We bypassed English bull terriers that had walked off the pages of a Dickens novel, and cooed over dotty-looking Dandie Dinmonts straight out of a Disney cartoon. At one point we were almost squashed by a massive, and massively disobedient, Neapolitan mastiff whose wrinkled face was clearly in need of Botox. Then we were washed by an overexuberant Bergamasco, an Italian Alpine dog whose eighteen-inch-long nose-to-tail dreadlocks made him look like an end-to-end Rastafarian.

We paused for a long while with Bert the Saint Bernard, a breed for which I've had a soft spot ever since I learned about the wonderful Swiss mountain-rescue dogs in geography lessons at primary school. Although an adult male can weigh up to two hundred pounds, Saint Bernards love small children — Joshua clambered all over Bert, but the dog took absolutely no notice of him — and, as his breeder explained, they don't need much exercise.

Bert was as big as an adult lion. I got down on my hands and knees to stroke his head, which was about three times as big as mine, and as he thumped his tail on the ground the whole of Earls Court seemed to vibrate. As I gazed into his large, red-rimmed, soulful eyes, tears of emotion sprang into my own. His size alone made his breed totally unsuitable for us — if Bert had lain down on our living room floor, he'd have looked less like a fur rug than wall-to-wall fitted carpet — yet there was something reassuring about his bulk that made me feel strangely tempted. Were there any drawbacks to owning a dog like him? I asked his proud owner. None, she said, if you didn't mind the molting and drooling. At home Bert usually wore a toweling bib to catch the constant dribble, and when she'd brushed him earlier that morning she'd filled a large carrier bag with loose hair. I really ought not to get so up close and personal with him in my black trousers and sweater, she advised.

It was too late. By the time Joshua and I left Bert's pen, we were drenched, covered with hair, and looked rather like wet white Yetis. No wonder that when the dogs set off to rescue lost mountain-climbers, they carried a barrel tied round their necks: it wasn't filled with reviving brandy, as I'd been taught at school, it was there to stop the people they rescued from drowning in dog saliva.

Our search for the perfect dog continued, but by now realism was setting in — for me, that was. Joshua ran from pen to pen, falling in love with cute little Labrador puppies one minute and fully grown Irish setters the next, while I followed behind trying to temper his enthusiasm with the voice of reason and doom. No, we couldn't have a greyhound, they needed too much exercise. Pugs snuffled too much, and so did boxers and Pekingeses. Dachshunds suffered from back problems. Like Bert the Saint Bernard, an Irish wolfhound was far too big for our flat, and the Pomeranian, however pert and pretty, was so small she'd get under our feet. No, it really wasn't fair to keep a New-foundland with webbed paws in a city when it was built to go swimming — it wouldn't even fit into our bath. And, yes, this tiny Rottweiler puppy did look adorable, but it'd look less so when it was a meter high, slavering on a chain, and had its teeth clamped round my throat.

All around us people were succumbing to doggie madness. Some were buying dried bulls' penises for their best friends to sink their teeth into — a meter long, and a snip at three pounds. Others were snapping up pink sheepskin dog coats, patent leather dog shoes, and couture collars covered with silver charms. One salesman tried to sell me a collapsible dog stroller, which looked awfully similar to the one I'd once pushed Joshua around in. It was perfect for taking your lazy pooch for a walk, he said. Its delicate paws need never touch the ground.

Joshua and I sat down for twenty minutes beside one of the show rings to watch the judging of the Waggiest Tail Competition. "I'm looking for a dog with a smile in its tail," said the judge, in all seriousness. This was followed by a performance of dog dancing — otherwise known as Heelwork to Music — after which we got up and resumed our search. As I turned up my nose at yet another breed (I think it was the Doberman) Joshua became tearful and I reached the end of my leash — I mean, rope.

It was time to go. Discover Dogs had taught me a valuable lesson: I didn't want a dog. I grabbed hold of Joshua's hand and dragged him toward the exit. But just before we got there, we stumbled across an exhibition stand overflowing with the most beautiful creatures I'd ever seen. Tumbling over each other excitedly, tails wagging madly, they ran about in their metal enclosure like lambs on speed. Varying in color from chestnut to black, white, and tan, they had long silky ears, the cutest round black noses, and huge, sparkling, soulful brown eyes. Joshua pulled free of my restraining grip and darted toward them. When they saw him coming, they bounded over to greet him on dainty, feathery paws. "Can I pet one?" Joshua begged the breeders.

The two men opened the gate to the pen and drew Joshua inside. Within seconds he was surrounded by a moving mass of glossy coats, smiling muzzles, and pink tongues. One little dog crawled onto his lap, another threw itself into his arms. Yet another jumped up and washed one of his ears.

"These aren't too big or too small for us, are they, Mum?" he said hopefully.

I shook my head. I had to admit that, at about twelve inches high, they were the perfect size, like Baby Bear's chair in the story of Goldilocks.

I, too, entered the enclosure, where one of the breeders gave me a young bitch to hold. Her name was Darling, and she snuggled up to me just as Joshua had when he was a baby. Turning her little head so that it rested under my chin, Darling licked my neck and gave me what I can only describe as a doggie cuddle. My heart began to melt.

I realized I was on the slippery slope to losing my freedom, so I put Darling down and then asked the men to tell me in detail about all the breed's bad points. They burst out laughing and assured me there weren't any. Though they were descended from hunting dogs, the little sweeties didn't need too much exercise. They were never aggressive. Despite their soppy appearance, they weren't stupid either but, on the contrary, clever and easy to train. Neither nervous nor bad-tempered, they were loyal, gentle, and affectionate. Far from being snappy with children, they adored them. In short, as one British monarch had discovered long ago, these were the ultimate lapdogs and made the ideal, trouble-free family pet.

I looked at the dogs crowding around my son, long ears flopping, eyes gleaming, tails wagging, pretty muzzles open in what looked like smiles. Joshua grinned up at me from among them. I hadn't seen him look so happy since before his father died.

"Mum, Mum, can we get one of these?" he pleaded. "Please, please, please!"

I took a deep breath. "Okay, darling," I heard myself say. "Of course we can."

There was no point in prevaricating; I knew when I was beaten. I'd met my canine nemesis — the Cavalier King Charles Spaniel.

FOUR

A few days later, I impulsively got on the phone to the Kennel Club and asked them to send me a list of registered Cavalier King Charles Spaniel breeders who currently had puppies for sale. One, a Mrs. Colman, lived near Henley, a town on the River Thames not far from where my parents had once had a house. I took this small coincidence as a good omen and called her. Yes, Mrs. Colman said, she had four pups, though at fourteen days old they wouldn't be ready to leave their dam for another six weeks. Still, they were being snapped up by future owners faster than half-price cashmere sweaters at a Harrods sale. The bitches had already gone, but two dogs were still available, so if I thought I might want to buy one, I should visit her straightaway and reserve one. And oh, Mrs. Colman added, she also had a five-month-old male that might be available. Then again, he might not. She wanted to keep him, but her husband wanted her to sell him.

Joshua and I set off for Henley the following Sunday. By the time we left home — he strapped into the back of our clapped-out car listening to a cassette of *Just William*, I in the driver's seat, nervously working my way through the bar of chocolate I kept hidden in the glove compartment — I had cold feet. Did I really want a dog when I already had so many responsibilities? I could picture Udi, shaking his head for once with disapproval. I could also hear my late father saying, "You must be *mad!*" Yes, I must be mad: even though I knew Joshua would love visiting the puppies, I'd made a huge mistake in bringing him with me to see them. If I changed my mind about getting one, he'd be incredibly disappointed.

"Remember, we're just going to *look* at the dogs today," I warned him, as we headed down the freeway toward Berkshire. "We may not like them."

I thought I heard him mutter, "Oh, yes, we will." But since this was quickly followed by "I can't hear you, Mum. I'm listening to *William*," I might have been mistaken. I glanced into the rearview mirror. Headphones clamped over his ears, Joshua was gazing out of the window, face impassive.

"Well, even if we do like them," I droned on, "they're far too young to leave their mother yet, so we won't be able to bring one home with us for at least another six weeks. Did you hear what I said, darling? You do understand, don't you?" He ignored me. "Joshua? Take those headphones off for a moment, darling, will you? JOSHUA!"

"What?"

"Look, you do understand that we *definitely* won't be bringing a puppy home with us tonight? So don't be too disappointed, will you?"

His lips curled into a scarily smug smile. "Don't worry, Mum. I won't be."

Mrs. Colman's cottage was impossible to miss. A stone Cavalier King Charles Spaniel stood on duty outside the garden gate. A Welcome plaque on the front door bore a picture of a smiling Cavalier's face. The brass door knocker was shaped like a Cavalier's head. The doormat was decorated with four Cavaliers — an auburn-coated "Ruby," a black-white-and-chestnut "Tricolour," a "Black and Tan," and a chestnut-and-white "Blenheim." There was also a Cavalier-decorated "Beware of the Dogs" notice beside the doorbell. My ring was greeted by a symphony of barks and yaps, and when the door opened, Joshua and I were engulfed in a tidal wave of shiny coats, sparkling eyes, and fast-wagging tails. Remembering "Beware of the Dogs," I grasped his hand, but we were only in danger of being licked to death.

With her twenty-five or so dogs and bitches shut in the kitchen along with her husband, the petite, pretty Mrs. Colman showed us into her living room, where a green marble clock decorated with a Cavalier's face ticked on a stone mantelpiece, next to several Cavalier-shaped picture frames containing photographs of Mrs. Colman's pets. Cavaliers grinned at us from the hand-embroidered cushions on the rather hairy sofas, and a pair of lamps made out of Staffordshire Cavalier figurines held pride of place on the side tables. Oil paintings of Mrs. Colman's winning champions, framed in gold, adorned the walls, with a pin board of winners' rosettes. The windowsills were dotted with Cavalier card holders, candlesticks, trivets, and trinkets. Even the doorknobs had Cavaliers painted on them.

Mrs. Colman sat us down with a cup of tea and a homemade chocolate cake and sang the praises of her pedigree pooches, then put me through the third degree. Did I have a criminal record? Had I ever been prosecuted for cruelty to animals? Did I have access to a garden with secure boundaries, and a puppy-proof room? Did we own any other pets? Was I out all day at work? Had I ever kept a dog before? Did I intend to buy it health insurance? What was my attitude to corporal punishment? Did my butcher have a good supply of fresh tripe? Next she presented me with a list of essentials I'd need to buy if she agreed to sell me one of her precious Cavaliers. It included a training cage, an exercise pen, baby gates for the stairs, a poop scoop, a dog bed, a fleecy blanket, a selection of soft toys and chew bones, a brush-and-comb set, a toothbrush, dog shampoo, nail clippers, stainless-steel food and water bowls, and a first-aid kit containing, at a minimum, tweezers, cold compresses, anti-diarrhea medication, a syringe, and a rectal thermometer. "I suppose you'd like to see the puppies now," she said.

Shaken by the thought of that rectal thermometer, I got slowly to my feet while Joshua bounded upstairs to the bedroom where the pups were kept. It was small and, like all the rooms in the cottage so far, decorated with Cavalier paintings. The dam — a chestnut-and-white Blenheim Cavalier — lay stretched out fast asleep on the pink candlewick cover of a single bed. She looked exhausted, as any mother of quadruplets had a right to be. Below her on the floor, her four offspring crawled blindly around in a blanket-lined box, eyes screwed shut, skin glowing pink beneath a thin covering of white hair. Though they looked identical to me, Mrs. Colman pointed to two and said they were the only ones still available. They had yet to open their eyes, she explained, or to develop their distinctive markings, but they would in time turn into beautiful Blenheims like their mother.

Warned not to pick them up, as they were too young to be played with, Joshua knelt down beside the box and stroked the mewing puppies. They were beautiful, he breathed. I can't say that I agreed. To me, they were like tiny fat white rats with long ears. "They're very small," I said. "They seem rather helpless."

Mrs. Colman gave a hearty laugh. "Puppies grow up very fast, dear. By the time you take one of these home, he'll be running all over the place, chewing everything and piddling in corners. Don't worry, he'll only need feeding four times a day by then. As for housebreaking, once you've learned to recognize his pre-potty pattern, you'll have him trained in no time at all."

I was about to run back to the car screaming "NO!" at the top of my voice when I remembered the older puppy Mrs. Colman had mentioned on the phone. Since he was five months old, wasn't he already house-trained? Mrs. Colman looked doubtful when I mentioned him. Yes, of course he was house-trained, she said, give or take the occasional accident, but the thing was she really didn't want to part with him. She had a particular soft spot for him; in fact, out of all her dogs he was her favorite. But her husband insisted that his head was far too big for the standard, which made him useless to breed from. And since he was useless, they didn't have space for him.

A useless, big-headed male. This sounded like a feminist joke to which the punch line was *Is there any other kind?* But did I want one as a pet? I asked if we might see this overgrown monstrosity before we went home. "Oh, I suppose there's no harm in you having a peek," Mrs. Colman said and, somewhat reluctantly, went down to the kitchen to fetch him.

I tore Joshua away from the puppies and headed for the stairs. As we started down them, an angelic vision appeared at the bottom and galloped up to greet us.

We stopped in our tracks. This Blenheim Cavalier was no swollen-headed monster.

He was quite simply the most beautiful dog I had ever seen. He had huge white paws, dappled chestnut-and-white markings, and a madly waving flag of a feathery tail. His eyes were as round and bright as head-lamps, and pale brown beauty spots freckled his delicately upturned, ski-jump nose. I swear his mouth was smiling at us; it gave him a heart-meltingly sweet expression. All the other Cavaliers I'd seen so far had been pretty, but compared to this five-month-old puppy they didn't come close. This young Blenheim was handsome — incredibly so. In fact, he had the kind of film-star looks that take your breath away.

Joshua and I sat down side by side on the half landing and introduced ourselves to George — for that, Mrs. Colman told us when she reappeared at the bottom of the stairs, was his name. He threw himself at us as if we were his long-lost best friends, licked our hands, trampled over our feet, and yapped an overenthusiastic and incom-prehensible greeting. Then, before I knew what was happening, he had clambered onto my lap, put his paws on my shoulders, and aimed his tongue at my lips.

When it came to seducing people, George was a fast worker.

"Oh, he's gorgeous!" I exclaimed.

I'd fallen in love at first sight before, though never with a dog. But within seconds of seeing this one, I'd had what the French call a *coup de foudre*. I was knocked out, irredeemably smitten. If George had an unusually big head — and for the life of me I couldn't see it — it was totally understandable, given his good looks.

As if sensing he'd already made a conquest of me, he turned his attention to Joshua, leaping from my lap onto his and licking the remnants of Mrs. Colman's chocolate cake from his chin. "Yuck!" said Joshua, turning his head away, while clasping the wriggling puppy to him. Thwarted, George turned his attention to my son's neck and methodically set about giving it the best wash it had had in years, his tongue working it over like a small pink flannel. My ticklish boy screamed with laughter, joy radiating from his face.

Mrs. Colman looked up at the three of us with a resigned expression. "Well, if you really, really wanted him . . . I suppose I *could* part with him," she said. "You can take him on trial, if you like. If you find you can't deal with him, bring him back next week."

I looked at her at the bottom of the stairs, tears in her eyes. I looked at Joshua, whose pleading expression was as intense as a full-on spotlight. I looked at George. He was as near perfect a puppy as I could imagine. Why, he was even house-trained! On top of that, his breeder had offered to have him back if we couldn't manage him. However, I knew that if George came home with us, that would be it. Nothing would have been crueler than letting Joshua have him only to take him away after a week. Hadn't he suffered enough loss in his life already?

I wished Udi was there so I could ask him what I should do. He'd been a font of good advice — particularly when I hadn't asked for it — but now, when I needed to hear his opinion most of all, he was horribly silent. Like it or not, I was now the only adult in this family, and I had to make a snap decision — a decision that would not only affect my son's happiness but also, perhaps, the next fifteen or sixteen years of my own life.

Should I take George or shouldn't I?

It was solely up to me.

Half an hour later, I drove back to London, polishing off the last of the glove-compartment chocolate as I worried about whether or not I'd made the right choice.

I glanced surreptitiously into the rearview mirror. Joshua was strapped into the backseat, listening to his *Just William* tape through his headphones, just as he had on the way down to Berkshire.

When I pulled up at the next traffic light, I looked over my shoulder. The latest addition to our family lay across Joshua's lap. Fast asleep and snoring gently, George was the picture of contentment.

And, for the first time since his father had died, so was my son.

FIVE

"Joshua," I said, waking him up after I'd parked outside our house when we got back in the early evening, "before we take George inside, there are just two rules I want to make clear. Number One: he's definitely not allowed on the furniture. Number Two: he's *not*, repeat *not*, allowed in our bedrooms at night."

Joshua nodded sleepily. At that precise moment he was so happy to have George in his arms that he would have agreed to anything I'd asked. Later I realized I should have added a few more rules to my list — not least that he had to pick up every piece of Lego he ever dropped on the floor in future, that he should never ask for a raise in his allowance, and that he should look after me in my old age.

Since I'd had no idea when we'd set out that morning that we'd be bringing a dog home with us, I was as totally unprepared as a woman who finds a baby on her doorstep. Apart from the small bag of dog food Mrs. Colman had given me to tide us over, I had absolutely nothing on her list of essentials — no training crate, no stainless-steel food bowls, no dog bed, no fleecy blankets, no emergency medical kit, and definitely no rectal thermometer. Since we didn't even have a leash, I had to carry George in from the car.

For the first time in ages, I didn't dread coming into the dark house. Like Joshua, I was too excited. And so was George. His world up till now had consisted only of the Colmans' cottage and garden. Here was a whole new universe to explore. After sniffing curiously around our open-plan kitchen for a few minutes, paying special attention to the crumbs on the unswept floor, he made his way through to the living room end, where he crawled under the coffee table and out the other side, then gave the fireplace a cursory inspection.

Then George's eyes alighted on our red velvet sofa. As if he recognized it, his mouth fell open in a toothy grin. Tail swishing briskly from side to side, he walked up to it, sat in front of it, and eyed it as longingly as if it were a juicy bone.

"I think he wants to jump up on to it,

Mum," Joshua breathed reverently.

"Well, he's not going to, is he? That's Rule Number One — remember, darling? *No, George! No!*"

George turned and looked at me, then eyed the sofa again, this time bending his back legs in preparation for an upward leap.

"No!" I growled, wagging my index finger for good measure. "*Not* on the furniture!"

"Mum! Don't shout at him!"

"I am *not* shouting!"

"Yes, you are!"

"I'm not, Joshua! I'm just being firm."

"No, you're not!"

Instead of making a happy atmosphere in the house, George was already causing Joshua and me to quarrel. But he couldn't have cared less. As we were soon to learn, George lived in a world of his own, a world in which everyone adored him and he could do no wrong. Besides, his mind was still on that sofa. Head cocked quizzically to one side, he planted his hindquarters back on the rug and gazed at me again, brown eyes gleaming with intelligence. I had the strangest feeling that he understood exactly what I meant. "Good boy!" I cooed. "Well done! *Not* on the furniture! Yes, that's right!" George was not only clever, it seemed, he was also obedient. It looked as though living with him wasn't going to be as difficult as I'd feared.

George turned away from me and eyed the sofa for a third time. A moment later, his back legs flexed like an Olympic athlete's on the starting line. Then he raised his front paws and leaped into the air, landing neatly on the center of the feather-filled seat cushions. He sat down and smiled up at us as if for approval, wagging his tail with small, quick, nervous movements.

"NO!" I yelled.

Joshua leaped to his defense again. "Don't tell him off, Mum! He's only just arrived! And don't make him move! He looks so nice sitting there!"

This was too true. Like his namesake King Charles II, holding court from his royal throne, George the Cavalier looked as if he belonged on a red velvet sofa — so much so that I hadn't the heart to turf him off. Instead, I sat down beside him and gave him a cuddle.

Unbreakable Rule Number One had bitten the dust — and George had been in the house for less than five minutes. There was always Rule Number Two, I reminded myself as he curled up between us and promptly fell blissfully asleep.

Perhaps I should have kept him awake,

because when it came to bedtime — our bedtime — George was anything but sleepy. I pondered for ages about where to put his bed — or rather the cardboard box lined with an old blanket that we'd improvised for the night. Eventually I decided on the upstairs bathroom, which was small, warm, and cozy, with a window that let in not only a little light from the street but a view of the stars.

As a member of a large pack of dogs, George had never slept alone before. Mrs. Colman had warned me that at first he was bound to miss his parents and numerous brothers, sisters, cousins, aunts, and uncles. She'd suggested I put a hot water bottle among his blankets to remind him of their body heat. So, at around ten thirty that night, I filled Joshua's old Winnie-the-Pooh hot water bottle, put it into the cardboard box, and attempted to tuck George in with it.

"Will he be all right by himself?" asked Joshua, doubtfully, as George clambered out of the box for a third time, dragging out Pooh by the ears. "What if something happens to him?"

"What can possibly happen to him? He's in the bathroom. And he's perfectly content here!"

Yes, George was content jumping in and out of his box. He remained that way until we shut the door on him. Thirty seconds later he let out a single, confused, piercing yelp. There was a pause. Then another yelp. This pattern continued for the next ten minutes or so with the regularity of a metronome while Joshua fretted outside the door. "He's lonely, Mum. He's unhappy. He's missing all the other dogs. Just think how you'd feel if it was you in there. We should let him out. Just for tonight. He can sleep with me."

I stuck to my guns. "No. We've got to start as we mean to go on. And George is *not* going to sleep in our bedrooms. Full stop."

"Why not?"

"Because it's a Rule. Because it's unhealthy."

"Why?"

I tried to think of all the reasons why it was unhealthy for dogs to sleep in their owners' bedrooms, but I couldn't come up with a single one. But by now I'd gone so far that it was too late to give in. "Because," I answered firmly.

"That's not a reason!"

"Let go of that door handle! You're not to let him out!"

"Then I'll sleep in the bathroom with him!"

After winning the resulting argument, if only by a slim margin, I tucked Joshua up in his own bed, read him a story to the sound of George's intermittent yelping, then went to our other bathroom to take off my makeup. Since the *Book of the Week*, being read on Radio 4, failed to drown the yelping upstairs, I retuned the radio to Capital, then to Classic, LBC, Kiss, and finally, XFM. Even loud rock music failed to dull the intensity of George's increasingly miserable wails.

I fell into bed. By now I was exhausted. The yelping continued for another twenty minutes, at the end of which I was convinced I'd made a terrible mistake in buying George. How could I have been so foolish as to think I could cope with a puppy, even a five-month-old one? Eventually Joshua appeared at my bedroom door in his pajamas. "I can't sleep," he said. "George's barking is keeping me awake."

"Me, too. Go back to bed. He'll stop soon, you'll see," I said, sounding far more convinced than I felt. "Puppies are like babies — if you leave them to cry for long enough, they eventually tire themselves out and fall asleep."

"Is that what you did to me when I was small? Let me cry myself to sleep?" Joshua regarded me with suspicion, as if he were building up a catalog of parental ill-treatment to tell his future shrink.

"Well . . . Not often," I admitted. "Not ever, actually." Despite plenty of advice to the contrary from the more experienced Udi, who'd already brought up Tabby and Hannah, I'd flown to Joshua's cot whenever he'd so much as whimpered. In fact, I'd sometimes hung over him when he was fast asleep, to reassure myself that he was still breathing.

Somewhat mollified, my nine-year-old climbed into bed beside me. After a while, George's yelping stopped. "See?" I said smugly. "I told you he'd settle down."

We lay side by side in silence, waiting for the protests to start up again. We waited and waited, but nothing happened. Eventually the silence grew even more disturbing than George's barking had been.

"Do you think he's all right?" Joshua said after what seemed like an hour but was probably five minutes. "Perhaps something's happened to him."

"Such as?"

"Maybe he's barked himself to death."

"Dogs don't bark themselves to death!" I

exclaimed, though when the silence started to ring ominously in my ears, I became anxious, too.

"Mum? Do something!"

"What? Look, he's probably asleep now. Go to sleep yourself. However," I relented, as anxiety overtook me, too, "if you're really, really worried, I'll look in on him quickly."

I crept upstairs on tiptoe, with Joshua close behind me. Making as little noise as possible, we put our ears to the bathroom door. There was an odd scuffling sound coming from inside, followed by a retching, gasping cough. Panicking, we threw open the door to be greeted by a blinding white snowstorm. In the middle of it stood George, in the process of regurgitating the remainder of the toilet paper roll he'd unraveled and shredded into tiny pieces. Delighted to see us, he threw himself at us, then lunged out of the door. By the time we'd cleared up the mess, he'd disappeared and wouldn't come back when we called him.

Eventually we found him in my bedroom, stretched out on his belly in the middle of the bed. His hindquarters were splayed out behind him like a pair of frog's legs, his ears were spread on either side of his head like Dumbo's, and his round black nose was tucked neatly between his front paws. He opened one eye when we came in, then quickly closed it. That glance told me everything: George wasn't going anywhere.

Unbreakable Rule Number Two had just gone the same way as Unbreakable Rule Number One. This was what passed for discipline in my home. I no longer had the spirit to fight him. After all, I reflected, it *was* George's first night in his new house, away from the large family of dogs he'd always known. And he was only a young puppy. I'd let things be tonight, and turn over a new strict leaf tomorrow. George obviously needed Joshua and me for comfort right now, just as much as we needed him.

Careful not to disturb the new arrival, we climbed into my bed, one on either side of him. With the warmth of his body permeating ours, we were soon fast asleep.

Six

I was awoken at six o'clock the next morning by a terrible hissing noise. In my semi-conscious state I presumed that it was caused by a leak from an industrial gas pipeline. Then I remembered there was no industrial gas pipeline running through my bedroom.

I also remembered something else: before the advent of George, our house had not been a pet-free zone.

We already owned a cat.

I opened my eyes. There she stood at the end of the bed, back arched, tail raised, her tiger-striped tabby fur standing on end like that of a cartoon animal plugged into an electric socket. Her lips were pulled back to reveal a mouthful of sharklike teeth, and her face was contorted into a wicked grimace. Yellow as a devil's, and flashing an intermittent terrifying red, her eyes were fixed on the canine usurper wedged into the space between Joshua and me.

Monster Mog had come home after one of her all-night binges. All hell was about to break loose.

You may wonder why I haven't mentioned our cat before. Well, the truth is that I did my best to forget about her. That isn't to say that I neglected her. I cared for her as diligently as I had all the other cats I'd owned: Peanut and Doorstop, the pair of stray lovers who'd jumped through my living room window and into my life some years earlier, one giving birth within days to a litter of five beautiful kittens; Izzie and Ozzie, the identical twins that, at my sister's insistence, I'd adopted from a local cat sanctuary — one agoraphobic, the other bulimic (too afraid to leave the flat, Izzie peed on the carpet, while Ozzie wolfed his food with undisguised greed then promptly threw it back up); and darling Gremlin, the tiny tortoiseshell to whom I'd been devoted despite, or perhaps because of, her countless neuroses (they included a terror of the vacuum cleaner and a profound fear of every human except me) and whom, to my dismay and lasting regret, I'd accidentally killed one night when she'd come running across the road to greet me as I reversed my car into a parking place.

Monster Mog was quite a different character from her predecessors, most of whom, like Gremlin, had met a grisly end on the London roads. ("You either coop them up in the house or let them out to have fun," a down-to-earth vet had told me after my second cat had fallen victim to a hit-and-run driver. "If I were you, I'd accept that it's best they lead a short but sweet life.") Unfriendly, violent, and with an untrustworthy, unpredictable temperament, Monster Mog was like the office bully: though she could be nice as pie to you some of the time, you never knew when she would turn on you. On the whole she was best avoided. Sometimes she'd curl up on your lap, purring contentedly as you stroked her. Then, without warning, she'd lash out with her talons and draw trails of blood down your arms. At other times, she'd jump onto your shoulder and gently nuzzle your ears, only to sink her fangs into your neck a moment later. Pick her up and Monster Mog would squirm to free herself. Put her down and she'd claw your legs on the way up and back into your arms. Unsuspecting visitors to our house, seduced by her benign Cheshire Cat grin, often fell prey to her unpredictable behavior, ignoring our warnings that they should be on their guard. I bore the scars of many encounters with her — a gash on my neck, tooth marks on the back of my wrists and ankles, and a small scratch dangerously close to my left eye.

I'd had Monster Mog since she was twelve weeks old. She was now five, and lived her own life. Though she always turned up at mealtimes, she disappeared through the downstairs cat flap immediately afterward with the selfish indifference of a moody teenager whose parents accuse her of treating their home like a hotel. And like a self-absorbed sixteen-year-old, she didn't give a damn what effect her behavior had on us, her family, for whom she appeared to feel nothing but a kind of sneering disdain. I'd stopped making excuses for her long ago. Friends had suggested that I find her a new home since she clearly didn't like ours, but I couldn't bring myself to. Despite her tricky nature, she was part of the family and we still loved her, Joshua in particular. Besides, she was my responsibility. Taking on an animal, I figured, was like taking on a life partner: you did so for better or for worse.

Naturally I'd told Mrs. Colman that we had a cat. Since she was unfazed by this, I'd expected George to react in the same way. In most homes — including that of our friends the Alwyns, whose menagerie of pets had inspired Joshua to ask me if we could have a dog — dogs and cats coexisted happily, and if Monster Mog played up, I was sure that one loud bark from George would put her in her place. After all, even at five months old he was bigger than she was. And he was a dog — traditionally the cat's worst enemy — so in any power struggle he was bound to have the upper hand.

How wrong could I have been? I'd forgotten to take into consideration Monster Mog's character, as well as the concept of territorial rights. Monster Mog was not only a monster, she'd occupied the house first. Though she'd been banned from our bedroom during Udi's lifetime — he hadn't been a cat lover — recently she'd started coming in to see me whenever she got home in the early hours, and she'd even taken to sleeping at the end of my bed. Unpleasant as she could be when she was awake, her presence had made me feel a little less lonely.

And, despite the continuing support I received from my family and friends, I was terribly lonely. It wasn't hard to fill the days with activity because I had a young child to look after, but the nights were a different matter. After Joshua had gone to bed, I'd sit alone in the living room and not know what to do with myself. I didn't like listening to music because it made me emotional, so I'd watch endless rubbish on television or leaf through my address book in search of someone different to telephone. I tried to read, but I couldn't concentrate for long on any book. Even newspaper or magazine articles didn't hold my interest.

The view from the sofa where I usually sat at night — where Udi and I used to curl up together — led through the archway into the kitchen and directly to the end of the table and what I still regarded as *his* chair. The sight of it depressed me. I'd remember Udi sitting in it, conducting one of his many long telephone conversations with distraught psychotherapy clients or his relatives in Austria; or leafing through *The Times Literary Supplement* or the Innovations catalog. Proof that this was perhaps my husband's favorite reading matter lay in the number of strange domestic gadgets we possessed. They included half a magnetic sponge kit for cleaning the outside of the windows from inside the house (the other half had fallen into our neighbor's hedge the first time we'd tried it out), a battery-operated sweater defuzzer that tore holes in our sweaters, and a large white plastic garlic peeler that looked like an instrument of torture and had splattered garlic shreds over the entire kitchen on the one occasion we had used it.

It was during those endlessly long evenings that I missed the things about Udi that had once driven me mad: his incessant smoking; his uncanny ability to move the goalposts whenever we discussed any serious issue; even a good old domestic row about my untidiness. Although other people told me how happy and fulfilled Udi had been with me, I also fretted, irrationally perhaps, that I hadn't been nice enough to him. Believe me, there's nothing like the death of your spouse to make you reexamine your past behavior and find it wanting. Like all those times when I'd sulked for days on end after some petty quarrel. Or when I'd insisted we spend our summer holiday with my parents in France instead of going to Spain, which Udi loved. The times when I hadn't paid him enough attention, or had stroked Monster Mog's ears instead of holding Udi's hand. The times when I'd caused a quarrel at the end of a perfectly nice evening by taking offense at some tactless remark Udi had made (and my dear late husband was an expert at those). Inevitably, the conclusion I reached was that I might have been an okay wife and partner, but I hadn't been good *enough,* particularly not for someone who was destined to die at the age of fifty-six and really ought to have had more fuss made of him while he was alive. Now, of course, it was too late to do anything about it. I couldn't make up for my past failures. I couldn't even apologize. I simply had to shoulder a shed-load of guilt and get on with the rest of my life.

After making myself feel thoroughly miserable, I'd turn off the living room lights, go downstairs to bed, and worry myself sick. It wasn't Udi's ghost that haunted me; I haunted myself. All my anxieties — about Joshua's happiness, money, the future — crowded in on me. Why had this happened? I asked myself time and again. In what ways would my son suffer from growing up without a father to guide him? Why had it had to be *my* husband who'd died? At the same time I knew I had no right to feel sorry for myself. Until the last two years had brought everything crashing down, I'd led something of a charmed life. Like one of Bridget Jones's "smug marrieds," I'd had a beautiful home, an interesting life, a husband who'd loved me, a wonderful extended family, a healthy child, and two lovely adult stepdaughters with whom I got on incredibly well. Though I'd lost my husband and my father, I still had so much. In addition, unlike many women in my position, I also had a secure roof over my head and enough money in the bank not to have to worry too much about paying the bills for another month or so.

But what would happen then? I'd never been particularly good at earning a living. My past career had been checkered, to say the least. Since dropping out of art college in my early twenties, I'd been in turn a temporary shop assistant, a temporary secretary (one who couldn't spell, do short-hand, or type), the untrained administrator of a revolutionary left-wing theater company, a trainee film editor at the BBC, a London tourist guide, a freelance journalist, and more recently, the author of four published novels and one history book, none of which had made the best-seller list. As a successful television producer, Udi had always earned far more than I did. How would I manage to sustain our comfortable lifestyle on my meager earnings?

Night after night thoughts like these kept me wide awake. I suffered from almost permanent insomnia, and in the early hours of the morning I'd call up friends in North America, who I knew would still be awake, and chat to them. When eventually I fell asleep, more often than not with the help of a sedative, I woke at the slightest sound. Though we lived in North London, less than a mile from some of the busiest roads in the metropolis, our street was amazingly quiet at night. So little traffic passed that I could hear owls hooting, the scufflings of foxes as they rooted through the garbage cans, even the cry of an occasional badger on Hampstead Heath. Often I'd wake up at four in the morning for no reason at all, having dozed for a couple of hours, and be surrounded by an absolute silence I found frightening and oppressive. Was this what it was like to be dead? I wondered morbidly. I can't say that finding Monster Mog curled up at the end of the bed provided any real comfort at these moments. Still, I was glad she was there.

This morning I wasn't so sure. She'd come home and, horror of horrors, found a large puppy lying in her usual place. Her hissing grew louder and louder, and since Joshua knew how vicious she could be, he was sitting bolt upright and looking at her fearfully. Meanwhile George, who knew no better, lifted his head out of the valley he'd created between us and regarded Monster Mog with the sort of mildly joyous expression a baby might adopt when encountering a brightly colored rattle. He'd obviously never seen anything like Monster Mog before, and he seemed to lack the normal anti-feline aggression. Instead of barking at her as another dog might have done, he stretched his pretty black nose toward her, sniffing her in a curiously delicate, almost polite manner.

Monster Mog was not impressed. She spat at him, then recoiled. George didn't get the message. Paw by paw, his flag of a tail waving slowly, he inched toward his new friend. She spat at him again. Surprised, but not dismayed, George wiped the spittle from his face with his right front paw and, presuming she was playing some sort of game with him, inched closer.

"Do something, Mum!" Joshua whispered. "Monster Mog might hurt him!"

"Don't worry," I said. "He's a dog. I'm sure he can sort this out by himself."

Just then Monster Mog sprang at George, and slashed his left ear with her right front paw. Instead of going for her, he yelped, turned tail, and dived for cover between Joshua and me. After a couple of minutes, his trembling nose poked gingerly out from under the duvet. He was terrified.

Still hissing loudly, our cat continued to glare at George as if she wanted to kill him.

Then, after a few minutes, her mouth curled into a disdainful sneer and she slipped off the bed with a dismissive snort. As she sauntered out of the room, she swished her stiff tail furiously in the air and treated us to a meaningful view of her backside.

SEVEN

Despite this inauspicious start, I believed naively that it would be only a matter of weeks before our cat and new dog came to some sort of understanding. They might never be bosom buddies, but they would soon grow fond of each other or, at the very least, learn to tolerate each other's presence. I was underestimating our cat.

My brother-in-law Philip felt sorry for Monster Mog. Though I did, too, I also knew that the situation was mostly of her own making. I'm afraid the contrast between her character and George's said it all. She was temperamental and difficult; he was sweet-natured and affectionate. While she treated us like inferior slaves, he followed us everywhere like an ingratiating court jester, even licking our feet when he got the chance. She was as aggressive as a pit bull terrier; he deserved the epithet "pussycat."

You couldn't help being wary of Monster

Mog, just as you couldn't help loving George. Gentle, cuddly, kindhearted, and playful, he was like a real live teddy bear, and Joshua was besotted by him. He took him for walks and wasted hour after hour playing chasing games with him and trying to teach him the basic commands — "Sit!" "Down!" and "Come!" He threw sheets over George's head and giggled as the dog had fun escaping from them. He watched George bark at his reflection in the mirrored wardrobe doors and try to get behind them to meet the dog on the other side.

Though the kind of squeaky plastic dog toys they sell in pet shops left George cold, paper in all its forms fascinated him. He devoured *The Guardian* faster than a group of left-wing liberals and caused havoc with the wrapping tissue in our local children's shoe shop. Luckily the manager was a dog lover. Far from minding about the paper shredding, she encouraged it.

A box of Kleenex was the best gift on earth to George: he ripped it apart, then shredded the contents, half of which he swallowed and later ejected from his rear end. He also destroyed more than one magazine article I was trying to write; but he looked so sorry when I told him off that I forgave him at once.

His favorite plaything was an improvised toy made of scrunched-up newspaper stuffed into an old sock. If Joshua dangled one in front of him, George would chase around the flat in pursuit of it, running up and down the stairs and trampling across everything in his path — sofas, chairs, the coffee table, newly made beds, human laps, even the outraged Monster Mog — regardless of the havoc he caused. Once he'd managed to wrest the stuffed sock from Joshua's grasp, he'd shake it with all the force of a lion killing its prey, then settle down quietly to disembowel it. By the time he'd chewed a hole through the fabric and fished out the innards, he was usually so exhausted that he fell asleep, his head cradled on piles of sodden newsprint.

I didn't mind clearing up whatever mess George caused, even the occasional puddle, for, like Joshua, I was devoted to him. He might not have won any prizes for intelligence, but he made my heart melt every time I looked at or cuddled him. Like a flower child of the 1960s, George loved everybody — from us, his owners, to the would-be burglar we surprised one afternoon attempting to break into the hall. His tail wagged constantly. Maybe it was a breed thing: there's a joke about Cavalier King

Charles Spaniels' tails. Mr. Smith takes his Cavalier to the vet and asks for its tail to be docked. "Why on earth do you want that done?" asks the shocked vet. "It's cruel, unnecessary, and painful! And Cavaliers are well known for their wagging tails! It's the way they express joy and affection." Mr. Smith shrugs his shoulders. "That's just it," he answers gloomily. "You see, my mother-in-law's coming to stay, and I don't want her to think that anyone's pleased to see her."

Of course, having George didn't stop us missing Udi, but he'd done what I'd hoped he would, which was to bring the fun back into our daily lives and make us feel a little more at peace with ourselves. No longer did we have to struggle to make conversation when we were alone together. We always had George to talk about. When Joshua came home from school, a playmate was always waiting for him: George. On weekends, we had a real reason to go for walks on the Heath: to exercise George. And when Joshua, my niece Jessica, and my stepgrandson Nathaniel built a castle in the living room with sofa cushions, sheets, and pillows, as they often did, they now had a proper prisoner to hold hostage inside it: George. When I sat alone on the sofa at night, with George stretched out asleep in front of the fire, I felt that our house was no longer a mausoleum but a real home again. For all these things I was eternally grateful to my Cavalier. I couldn't stop making a fuss of him.

Nor could anyone else, it seemed. Strangers stopped Joshua in the street to admire George whenever he took him out for a walk. Children queued up to stroke him outside the local school. Adults of both sexes stooped to kiss him and addressed him in the same oochy-coochy tones they might have used to a baby. As for the rest of the family, they, too, were mad about George, including my ninety-four-year-old grandmother, Laura, and my mother, Honey, who'd never quite got over losing Freddy, the Yorkshire terrier we'd had when I was growing up.

As for Sue . . . A healthy sibling rivalry had always existed between my sister and me, and more often than not she'd had the upper hand. Her glowing school reports — "First-class work!" "Excellent!" "Yet another successful term!" — had always put mine in the shade, though that wasn't difficult when the best my teachers could say about me was that I was lazy, slapdash, and hadn't yet reached some mythical and never-achieved "full potential." When it came to men, my extremely attractive sibling had had boys queuing up to date her ever since she'd turned thirteen, while I'd languished alone, forever pining over some lank-haired character who didn't know I existed. Later Sue's career as a top newspaper journalist and arts editor had outstripped my own working life, as had her earning power. Now, at long last, I'd got one up on her. "How *could* you get him?" she gasped when she came round to see George for the first time. "You *know* he's *exactly* the kind of dog *I've* always wanted!"

At least Sue and I could express our sibling rivalry in words, then laugh it off. Not so Monster Mog. Like Cerberus guarding the gates to the ancient Greek underworld, she sat on the middle step of the stairs, barring George's way up or down. If he barked at her, she spat at him. If he tried to walk past her, she boxed or clawed him, often drawing blood. After a while I began to wish that George would take a run at her with bared teeth. Just one show of canine aggression, I felt sure, would be enough to cure her of this dreadful habit. But though George had nerves of steel when it came to hearing fireworks or being shot at by cap guns, in standing up to Monster Mog he proved a complete wuss. Instead of going for her when she threatened him, he trembled in the downstairs hall or cringed on the top step yelping for someone to come and get him. Since Joshua was often at school, this was usually me.

Though I was trying to write another novel, I now found myself on full-time pet rescue duty, running up and down stairs at least fifty times a day, trying to coax George to run past Monster Mog, or moving her to one side so that he could squeeze by her, or, as a last resort, lifting him over her head while she tore at my ankles.

At the same time as she was tormenting the canine in our midst, Monster Mog was also attempting to make amends for her bad behavior toward us humans. Placatory gifts appeared in unexpected places: croaking frogs on the rug in the living room; a fat slug in the bath; half a pink worm writhing in the hallway; a giant moth in the kitchen, fluttering helplessly on chewed-up wings; and a selection of mice, some alive and kicking, others decapitated. Though I knew she meant well, I found it hard to appreciate these unsolicited offerings.

Three months after joining the family, George continued to yelp if left in the bathroom at night. Consequently, he still slept in my bedroom. I'd bought him a snug bed made of fake fur, the kind any normal designer dog would be delighted to curl up in, and put it in the corner of my room, but he refused to get into it. Like his ancestors, King Charles II's spaniels, my Cavalier preferred to spend the night on a proper double bed alongside his owner. Not just alongside her, actually, but practically on top of her.

Through force of habit I still lay on the extreme right-hand side of the mattress, which I'd always occupied when Udi was alive. The other side — his — still felt sacrosanct: as with the chair at the end of the kitchen table, I'd have felt I was trespassing if I'd moved into it. George had no such qualms. He started off the night stretched out on the flat space where Udi's feet had once been and, by almost imperceptible degrees, he worked his way slowly upward. At midnight, his nose would hover inches from my ankles, but by one a.m. his upper body would be pressed against my knees. By two, we'd be back to back, by three his whiskers would be tickling my armpit, and I'd often wake at seven in the morning to find his nose and front paws lying heavily across my chest, just inches from my neck.

Not to be outdone, Monster Mog followed suit on my other side. Though the super-king-size bed was six feet wide, I could now occupy only a narrow eighteen-inch strip of it. I was in no-man's-land, sandwiched between two enemies. In sleep, a truce existed between them, but I hardly dared turn over or move my legs in case the aggressor woke up and went on the rampage. Somehow it never occurred to me to turf off either or even both of my pets. Little wonder that I suffered from terrible insomnia.

Early one morning this uncomfortable situation came to a gory head. After spending several hours of fretful wakefulness squeezed between my bedfellows, I finally managed to knock myself out with the aid of a sleeping pill. What seemed like only seconds later I woke up with a start, aware of a strange rustling sound close by.

My immediate thought was that an intruder had broken into the flat. I glanced at my bedside clock: it was three forty-five a.m. Straining my ears, I listened in terror. There was the rustle again! I squinted into the darkness. George was awake, lying parallel to my left leg. Monster Mog was sitting on my right. Both were facing away from me, and their tails were swishing. In an unusual show of togetherness, both were inching forward, paw by paw.

There was someone — or something — at the end of my bed.

I switched on the light in one quick — incredibly courageous — movement. With a gasp I beheld the intruder sitting on the end of the duvet. It was a bloody mouse. By which I mean it was a mouse, and it was bleeding. One of its back legs had been chewed half-off. The tiny creature, with its pinhead eyes, dirty brown fur, long tail, twitching nose, and gaping wound looked shocked and horrified, as well it might under the circumstances. It wasn't, however, half as shocked and horrified as I was.

I leaped out of bed with a scream. Monster Mog glanced at me and licked her cheeks, which were lipstick red, as was the trail of bloodspots on my bedroom carpet. She must have gone out on the prowl while I was asleep, caught the mouse, brought it in through the hall cat flap, and deposited it on my bed as a present for me. I felt about as grateful as an animal rights activist who'd been given a fur coat for her birthday. Thanks a lot, I felt like saying. Now please take the damn thing back.

Unwanted, unimaginably scared, and under surveillance by two hungry-looking giants, the mouse lurched toward the edge of the bed in search of an escape route, only to find itself stranded. Both giants shifted in pursuit of it. Monster Mog got there first and brought her right front paw down hard on the little skull, pinning it firmly to the bloodstained white duvet cover. The cat-and-mouse game continued for a few minutes while I flapped around uselessly. If only Udi were here! I thought. He'd know exactly what to do! But Udi wasn't there. Of course he wasn't! If he had been, we wouldn't have had George, Monster Mog would never have been allowed in the bedroom, and the mouse wouldn't be there either.

This was no time for regrets. I had to rescue the bleeding rodent before Monster Mog killed it or — worse — it did a runner. I don't have a phobia about mice: living in an apartment infested with them during my art student days had cured me of that. But I certainly didn't want to see the poor little creature torn to pieces in front of me, and neither did I want it limping around my house, then curling up and dying under my bed. I grabbed the nearest thing I could find — my white terry-cloth dressing gown — grappled Monster Mog out of the way, and threw the robe on top of her victim. Gathering it up in the pale, soft folds, I carried it toward the cat flap, my pets barking and mewing at my heels. My plan — such as it was — was to push the robe through the flap, release the mouse, then lock the cat flap from the inside so that Monster Mog and George couldn't get out. This would give it a fighting chance of survival.

Unaware that I was selflessly trying to rescue it, the mouse squealed and squirmed inside its increasingly bloody terry-cloth prison, as scared of me as it was of the two other species it had just encountered. As I got down on my knees beside the cat flap, it squeezed out of my tightly cupped hands, disappeared down the robe's sleeve, then emerged a split second later from under the hem. Like lightning on its three and a half legs, it darted across the hall and disappeared beneath a tall, heavy Victorian bureau.

"Get back!" I shouted, as George and Monster Mog dashed forward and scrabbled wildly at the bottom of the bureau with their claws. I lay down next to them, nose to nose, and peered into the dark crack between the carpet and the bureau's base to see the escapee cowering at the rear.

Suddenly Joshua's bedroom door opened and a pale-faced, sleepy figure emerged. "What's the matter?" he cried, seeing all three of us lying on the floor by the desk with our noses pressed to the ground. I was so used to protecting him from things I thought might scare or upset him that I sat up and said automatically, "Nothing!"

He rubbed his eyes. "I woke up 'cause I heard noises. Why are you lying on the floor in your pajamas? Are you hurt?"

"No, no! Everything's fine. Go back to bed. I've, um, just dropped something and I'm trying to find it."

"Yeah, right! In the middle of the night?"

I'm a hopeless liar. The truth was soon out. Far from being upset, Joshua rose magnificently to the occasion. Displaying a degree of organization that would have done justice to his father, he shut George in my bedroom and Monster Mog in the study, then ran up to the kitchen in search of the Reusable Animal-friendly Mousetrap he remembered Udi had once ordered from an Innovations catalog. For the past three years this had languished under the sink alongside the Innovations Everlasting Brass Polish ("Everlasting" because it was never opened), a Remote-controlled Cooking Thermometer, for which we'd never acquired the right batteries, and an Automatic Soap Dispenser with Built-in Musical Chimes, still in its original box.

Now, at long last, one of these gadgets was about to come into its own. After baiting the trap with a piece of chocolate, Joshua and I prodded it under the bureau with the help of a ruler. Still lying on the floor, but at a distance, we waited for ages until, attracted by the irresistible aroma of Cadbury's Fruit & Nut, the invalid limped into the small black plastic tube and the trap's door clicked shut.

I retrieved the trap, threw a coat over my pajamas, shoved my feet into some sneakers, went outside into the dark, rainy street, and released the mouse to an unknown fate some fifty yards from the house. When I returned home, I let the yelping dog and yowling cat out of their respective prisons, forced my overexcited son back to bed, stripped my duvet of its bloodstained cover, and shoved it into the washing machine with my dressing gown. By the time I'd remade my bed and crawled back into it, it was past five. Within minutes I'd been joined again by my animal companions who, worn out with the excitement, sank into a deep sleep, one on either side of me. I'd kick them out of the bedroom tomorrow, I promised myself. I was too tired to do battle with them right now.

The night's excitement was far from over.

Just as I was drifting off, I heard scuffling in the front garden, followed by a loud series of shrieks, as if someone was being strangled. Monster Mog leaped to her feet, back arched, and George started to bark like a maniac. I jumped out of bed, lifted the blind, and looked up to the street from my basement window just in time to see a large dog fox and vixen slink away over the garden wall. But, as I was about to discover, they, too, had left a special present for me: one had sprayed all over the window. A moment later, my bedroom filled with an unbearably strong, skunklike smell.

I put on my coat and sneakers again, this time accessorized with a pair of fetching yellow rubber gloves. Clutching a bucket of hot water laced with disinfectant, I went back out into the darkness and rain, clambered down the slippery grass slope of the front lawn, and scrubbed my bedroom window clean.

Despite my efforts, the foul stench lingered when I fell back into bed again. It was almost time to get up. Stuck back in no-man's-land, I stared up at the ceiling in despair. I wasn't against a bit of wildlife in the bedroom, but not of this kind.

The situation was out of control. Animals had taken over my home.

And one in particular was about to take over my life.

EIGHT

As a journalist and author, I knew about the importance of doing research. For a writer it meant finding out about your subject before you put a word on paper. It provided the architecture of your book or article, as well as the bricks and mortar. It was the skeletal framework upon which you hung the flesh of your story. If you did your research properly, you could sort out which facts were relevant and how many you could junk. You knew where you were going and how you were going to get there. In other words, you knew where you were.

On the other hand, if you'd done your research badly, or had skipped it, you were like a train that had come off the rails. You were out of control and hadn't the foggiest idea where you were headed or — this is particularly relevant here — how much of your precious time the journey would take.

Since I was well aware of all this, it might

seem odd that I hadn't delved into what it was like to care for a pedigree Cavalier King Charles Spaniel before I'd bought one. As far as I was concerned, a dog was a dog. You fed it, you gave it fresh water, you kept it warm, you took it on frequent walks, and you lavished it with love. I had no idea that Cavaliers were in any way special: how fussy they could be about their diet; how often you'd end up taking them to the vet; how troublesome their teeth were; and how generally exhausting one could be.

Or maybe the problems that arose soon after George joined the family were nothing to do with Cavaliers in general. Maybe the problem was George.

Out of all her beautiful Cavaliers, he had been Mrs. Colman's favorite. So before she'd allowed me to carry him away over her threshold, she'd naturally sat me down in the Museum of Cavalieriana that was her living room and given me the lowdown on the basics of looking after him. He needed to be brushed n times a week, she said, and fed x times a day on fresh tripe, dog biscuits, and meal, to which I should add half the contents of a garlic capsule. Every few days I'd have to y and z George. Inoculations, vaccinations, claw care, personal hygiene, behavior training, toilet training, tooth descaling . . . I tried to concentrate on what she was telling me, but I was so overwhelmed by the grown-up thing I'd just done — I'd bought a dog! — that it all went over my head.

It took me a few weeks, and an old book on Cavaliers, which I found in our local secondhand bookshop, to grasp what I'd landed myself with. A Cavalier was no ordinary dog, it turned out. It was a high-maintenance creature — the Victoria Beckham of pedigree pooches. I'm not talking about shopping here. To date, my George doesn't possess a single item of clothing. He has no fleecy hoody to keep him warm on chilly autumn days; no diamanté-encrusted tracksuit in which to wow the bitches at training classes; no faux-leopard-skin steel-spiked collar to impress on other dogs his manly credentials; and no canine Jimmy Choos to protect his precious paw pads from the unforgiving London pavements. Why, George doesn't even own a fur-lined parka with removable sleeves, matching cap, and coordinating fur-trimmed dog galoshes for those wet muddy walks on the Heath! All he has is what he stands up in: his own, rather disheveled coat, an extendable leash, and a plain black nylon expandable collar (expandable so that it can be loosened on his plumper days). Compared to some dogs — I'm thinking in particular of a petite Italian greyhound I once met in South London who had seven real pearl chokers and a wardrobe twice as large as my own, full of handmade designer outfits — you could almost say that poor George is deprived.

No, when I say high-maintenance, I'm talking about the amount of attention he required on a day-to-day basis. George, it turned out, was as time-consuming as a new baby. And not just any baby. A royal baby. For, like his ancestors, George had blue blood. Originally known as the English Toy Spaniel, and probably bred by crossing Spanish hunting dogs with tiny Oriental lap-dogs such as the Tibetan "palace" spaniel and the Japanese chin, dogs almost identical to George had been favorite pets at the royal courts of Europe since time immemorial. You can spot them in countless old works of art, looking just as aristocratic as their owners. There's one jumping up at its mistress in the fifteenth-century French Arras tapestry *The Offering of the Heart,* another curled up fast asleep in Titian's 1538 portrait of the Duchess of Urbino, and a pair sitting quietly at the feet of "Bloody" Queen Mary and her husband Prince Philip of Spain in a double portrait by Antonio Moro, which was painted in 1554, the year of the couple's marriage.

Not for nothing were the little dogs known as "comforters" in those days. Bred as pets as well as small hunting dogs, they kept their owners warm by sitting on their laps in the chilly palace halls, and lay under their feet on long, freezing coach journeys. At night they curled up with their masters or mistresses in their feather beds, where they proved not only more cuddly than brass warming pans filled with hot coals, but also a lot safer: however excitable a toy spaniel was, there was little chance of it setting the linen on fire.

"Spaniell gentle or comforter — a delicate, neat and pretty kind of dog . . . chamber companions, pleasant play fellows" was how Dr. John Caius, Queen Elizabeth I's physician, described the English Toy Spaniel in his 1570 essay, "De Canibus Britannicis," in which he listed every breed of dog known in the country at the time. But the comfort that toy spaniels provided was more than physical. In a world where you might see a parent divorced, disgraced, or even beheaded — a world in which you couldn't trust your closest relative and where, if you didn't play your cards right, you might even be put to death yourself — the pretty dogs with their sweet little snouts and silky coats proved the most steadfast and loyal of companions.

When Mary Queen of Scots was executed at her cousin Elizabeth I's behest at Fotheringhay Castle on February 8, 1587, her small black-and-white spaniel accompanied her to the scaffold; after her head was chopped off, the traumatized dog was found hiding under her blood-spattered petticoats. Sixty years later, when Mary's ill-fated grandson, King Charles I, was being pursued by Oliver Cromwell's Roundheads, he took refuge at Carisbrooke Castle on the Isle of Wight with his own toy spaniel, Rogue. The following January, 1649, Charles was condemned to death for high treason, and on the thirtieth of that month, the morning of *his* execution, he took Rogue for a final walk across London's Green Park to the scaffold, which had been erected outside the Banqueting Hall at Whitehall Palace. Sometime during that day, Rogue was dog-napped by the victorious Roundheads and touted around the city, as potent a symbol of the toppled monarchy as his late master's severed head.

Exiled in France, a country whose own royal family also favored the English Toy

Spaniel, Charles I's children continued his love affair with the breed. The late king's son and heir, the as yet uncrowned Charles II, was obsessed with them. When the thirty-year-old monarch-in-exile returned to England in May 1660, his favorite toy spaniel accompanied him and was rowed ashore from the royal ship in the same boat as the courtier and diarist Samuel Pepys. "I went, and Mr. Mansell and one of the King's footmen, with a dog that the King loved (which shit in the boat, which made us laugh and me think that a King and all that belong to him are but just as others are)," Pepys recorded graphically.

A large pack of the spaniels accompanied Charles II everywhere he went from then on, even to government meetings, where he passed the tedious hours by messing around with them. "All I observed there was the silliness of the King," Pepys observed, of one such meeting in Whitehall, "playing with his dog all the while, or his codpiece, and not minding the business." The dogs seemed to take "the business" more seriously than he did, according to the poet Lord Rochester, who wrote that the king's "very dog at Council Board, Sits grave and wise as any Lord."

Whitehall, St. James's, Hampton Court —

all the royal palaces were Liberty Hall as far as the royal spaniels were concerned. They ran riot in the corridors, slept on the silk-covered chairs, and relieved themselves freely on the floorboards and rugs. With their master, the king's, blessing, the bitches even gave birth and suckled their young in his bed. According to writer John Evelyn, all this "rendered it very offensive, and indeed made the whole Court nasty and stinking." Charles couldn't have been immune to the smell: in 1662 he employed George Russell, his sergeant of hawks, to take his spaniels out for exercise.

After 1689, when Charles's younger brother and successor, James II, was deposed in favor of his daughter and son-in-law, Mary II and William of Orange, the toy spaniel's place as royal top dog was usurped by a Dutch import: the squashed-nosed, bulbous-eyed pug. Crossbreeding of pugs, and maybe even bulldogs, with the toy spaniel eventually produced a hybrid with a dome-shaped head, long ears, protruding eyes, and the kind of flat nose and truncated muzzle that made it look as if it'd been in a collision with a palace privy. This was the forerunner of today's English Toy Spaniel, as it is known in the United States, a breed that, in Britain, was officially named the

King Charles Spaniel in 1923.

Yet these dogs were quite unlike those with which Charles II had once been besotted. Instead of flat heads and long muzzles, they typically had the domed skulls and squashed noses of the pug crossbreeds developed in William and Mary's time. In fact, the old-style features were considered highly undesirable until a New Yorker named Roswell Eldridge took it upon himself to reintroduce them. In 1926 Eldridge placed an advertisement in the catalog of Crufts Dog Show, offering a prize of twenty-five pounds — a large amount in those days — for long-nosed "Blenheim Spaniels of the Old Type, as shown in the pictures of Charles II's time." Within two years, Eldridge's idea had taken off in a big way, and the old-style spaniel had reappeared under the name *Cavalier* King Charles.

Three hundred years of royal inbreeding, my book on Cavaliers informed me, had ensured that the breed's teeth were prone to decay. So, like the present Prince of Wales, my "Charlie" was going to need help with his dental hygiene. Not just someone to squeeze the toothpaste onto the brush for him, either, but someone to clean his teeth for him every day for the rest of his life. And who was that going to be?

A Cavalier's eyes were often weepy. Like teeth, this was a breed thing, and nothing to do with his being unhappy. To ensure that he didn't pick up an eye infection, the owner should wash his eyes once a day with cotton wool and a little diluted Optrex. And since most Cavaliers liked having their faces cleaned, too, the owner might as well do that at the same time.

Still on the subject of washing, the book said that a Cavalier's long ears needed to be cleaned inside and out at least once a week, and the ear canals regularly checked for canker, wax buildup, and ear mites. It called for the occasional bath in special dog shampoo and daily grooming, preferably with an expensive real-bristle Mason Pearson hairbrush of the kind I'd always been too frugal to buy for myself. The preliminary brushing should always be followed by a going-over with a fine-toothed steel comb, to establish that no tangles or mats remained in the coat. And if a Cavalier got *very* muddy on the twice-daily walks he needed, the owner must towel off the excess mud, leave him to dry, then restore the shine to his coat by polishing him with a chamois leather or, alternatively, a silk handkerchief.

A Cavalier's claws grew very fast, the book went on. They must be trimmed with special nail clippers at least every other week. The hair underneath the paws often grew fast, too, and needed regular cutting with small scissors if the animal wasn't to slip on wooden floors and possibly injure himself. After every walk the Cavalier owner should check between the dog's manicured claws to make sure that no grass seeds, mud, or ice balls were stuck there, for these might aggravate the Cavalier's sensitive skin and start an eczema flare-up.

Had I seen my Cavalier "scooting" along on his rear end or licking his bottom? the book's author asked. Yes, I had to admit that I had. In that case, she suggested, my Cavalier might have worms. On the other hand, it could be that his anal sacs were bothering him. What on earth were anal sacs? I wondered — needlessly, as it turned out, for the author was about to tell me in more detail than I wanted to know. Situated just inside the rectum of every dog, the anal sacs, or glands as they were sometimes known, normally emptied themselves when-ever a dog defecated or was very frightened. In Cavaliers, however, the sacs sometimes needed a little . . . how shall we put it? Prompting. In other words, they had to be manually cleared. This could either be done with a strategically placed tissue and a squeezing movement outside the dog's bottom (the author provided an enlightening photograph here) or internally, using a lubricated and gloved finger inserted into the rectum (of this there was an incomprehensible cross-section diagram, similar to the ones that had put me off sex in a biology class at school). Though the procedure was messy and smelly, the author conceded, it wasn't hard for the Cavalier owner to master it. One's local vet could probably show one how to do it.

Since this particular Cavalier owner had no intention of ever learning how to empty her dog's anal sacs, it was high time she registered her puppy at the veterinary practice where she had previously taken Monster Mog. Weighing in at just over five kilos, George was a perfect specimen of a slim young Cavalier King Charles Spaniel, Greg the vet pronounced on our first visit. Luckily, George appeared to be in perfect health, and to have none of the heart, hip, knee, or eye problems that were endemic to the breed. The only problem Greg could anticipate was George's diet. "Atrocious" was how he described the tripe and puppy meal the breeder had recommended. Instead, he suggested that I should start George on one of the new, premium-grade, all-in-one dry dog foods that were now available. It might take him a little time to adjust to it — I should be prepared for protests, and even diarrhea — but in the long run it was well worth persevering.

By the time we left the vet's, George had had his anal sacs emptied by a nurse in a back room far away from me, and I was carrying a treasure chest of pharmaceutical and other goodies which included dog worming tablets, dog anti-flea sprays, beef-flavored all-in-one premium dry dog food, chicken-flavored dog toothpaste, a dog toothbrush, a dog hairbrush, a dog comb, dog shampoo, dog conditioner, a dog seat-belt for the car, some dog treats, and a bag of fluoride-impregnated dog dental chews. You name it, if it had the word "dog" in front of it I'd just bought it.

After visiting the vet, I was determined to take my responsibilities as a dog owner seriously. Looking after my Cavalier now dominated my life. Never mind Joshua or my work, George was my new full-time occupation. The first thing I did every morning was to put him out into the back garden. Next, I went upstairs to the kitchen, filled his water bowl with fresh water and his food bowl with a generous helping of all-in-one dry dog food. Of course George refused to touch it. The first time I'd offered it to him, he'd given it a cursory sniff then thrown himself down on the kitchen floor and glared up at me reproachfully. He'd been on a hunger strike ever since.

Naturally, George accompanied Joshua and me on the walk to school, when Joshua held the lead as proudly as the owner of any champion Cavalier in a show ring. But George didn't behave like a show dog. Nose pressed to the ground, he turned over every bit of filthy debris he found in the hope of finding something edible, a clear message that he would literally rather eat rubbish than the hard dry pellets he was getting at home. At least once en route, we had to prize open his jaws and remove some potentially lethal, moldy old bone or gummy sweet he'd snaffled up from the gutter. At least twice Joshua and I tried to look invisible while George pooped, usually in a most inconvenient spot, such as the middle of the pavement or halfway across a busy road. Though little seemed to be going into the front end of George, an awful lot still seemed to be coming out at the back.

"Do you *have* to pick it up, Mum?" my son complained, as I scooped up the dog mess with one of the many plastic bags that now distended my coat pockets. "Can't you just leave it on the ground like everybody else does?"

At least five or six times more on the way to school we had to stop to let George water the street furniture. On the day we'd brought him home from Mrs. Colman's, he'd been more or less house-trained, but during his first few weeks with us the "less" part of that statement had taken precedence and there had been puddles everywhere. After consulting my Cavalier book, I'd spent many hours loitering beside the local lamp-posts with him, murmuring encouraging endearments such as "Empty!" and "Be *good!*" while trying not to look like a sex worker soliciting clients. Luckily George soon cottoned on again to the joys of outdoor urination. And since the book recommended giving one's dog a great deal of positive reinforcement, whenever he lifted his back leg we praised his achievement so highly you'd have thought he'd just won the Nobel Prize.

There was soon no stopping George. After the first lamppost and the resulting flood, it was off to the next to release a mini-shower, and from there to a brick wall for a tiny trickle, and thence to a tree for . . . well, for nothing. Obviously he couldn't yet distin-guish between a meaningful act and an empty gesture, because he insisted on lifting his leg against every vertical surface we passed regardless of need. Each time he wagged his tail and grinned up at us, eyes gleaming with pride. "Well done, George, well done!" we cooed, to the bemusement of passersby who happened to glance at the bone-dry pavement. This wasn't doing my street cred much good.

There were other downsides to taking George with us on the walk to school. First, the journey that had formerly taken twenty minutes now easily stretched into a good three-quarters of an hour, what with all the stopping and starting, poop-scooping and praising we had to do. Second, I was becoming increasingly unpopular in the neighborhood. It wasn't enough that I diligently poop-scooped. No, judging from the disapproving looks I was getting, it seemed that allowing my dog merely to urinate in the street was regarded by some as an antisocial act on a par with lighting a cigarette on a maternity ward.

I'd always thought we British were a nation of dog lovers. The opposite now seemed to be true. In France, dogs still dined at the best restaurants. In the United States, canine day spas were opening every week. In Melbourne, Australia, restaurateurs were even planning to open a canine cappuccino bar. But in Hampstead, Northwest London, my George was banned from cafés, restaurants, shops, and even, inexplicably, the post office. In fact, I soon discovered that it was impossible to do any domestic chores when George was with me. One day I made the mistake of taking him into Brent Cross shopping mall, where I'd stopped on the spur of the moment to buy some much-needed lightbulbs. As I carried him into the lighting department, the security men appeared so quickly, and in such force, that you'd have thought I was transporting a live rattlesnake. I protested that there was no "No Dogs" sign at the entrance, and that George was doing no harm; in fact, since he was tucked under my arm, he wasn't even standing on the floor. But it did no good. If I wanted to take my pooch shopping, I was told sternly as I was escorted out by two burly men, it had to be in their "Peter Jones" store in Sloane Square, Chelsea. Apparently there was a special dog dispensation there so that the queen's corgis could go shopping with her. The Peter Jones staff kept a ledger wherein they recorded the name of any canine customer that disgraced itself. It was just like football, actually: two fouls and they were out for good.

Man's best friend was slowly being criminalized. What was a dog owner to do to avoid feeling like a social pariah? I began to think I should carry a mop and bucket around Hampstead with me so that I could clean up after George had piddled. That ought to pacify the snooty neighbors. Or perhaps I should put him in nappies. I don't think he would have taken kindly to his nether regions being clamped into Pampers. All that wadding would have interfered with leg lifting, and leg lifting, as we told him constantly, was *good.* As far as he was concerned, the world was now his personal urinal, and he intended to make full use of it.

Since it was impossible to do any shopping when he was with me, I took George straight home after I'd dropped off Joshua at school, and then I walked back into the village alone to buy food. When I got home for the second time, I put on George's leash again, this time to take him to the Heath for a run. Back home for the third time half an hour later, I stuck him in the bath, showered the mud off his paws, and settled down to groom him. Once a week I gave him a proper bath and dried him with my hairdryer. On other days I simply wiped his eyes and face with diluted Optrex, then carefully checked between his paw pads to make sure there were no stuck grass seeds. After that, I brushed and combed him while Monster Mog stood by, hissing and spitting. In the hope of placating her, I sometimes brushed her, too. But it made little difference to her mood, and the only thanks I ever got was a bitten finger.

After grooming his coat, it was time to deal with George's oral hygiene. This was a task I hated, mostly because he hated it, too. The moment he saw his toothbrush come out of the bathroom cupboard, he ran behind the sofa, clamped his mouth shut, and refused to open it. I cajoled, I coaxed, I pulled George out from his hiding place, held him down, and like a prison warden trying to force-feed a suffragette, attempted to squeeze the head of the tiny brush between his little teeth. I counted myself lucky if I got it past his lips. Though he never snapped or even growled, George stubbornly refused to cooperate. I soon realized that I was a dead loss as a dental hygienist and gave up trying. It was a relief to both of us. His teeth would have to look after themselves.

It was usually past midday when I finally went into my study and settled down to try to write an article. But, as with a new baby, when George was around it was impossible to concentrate on work for any length of time. There was my pet rescue duty on the stairs. And it was soon time for more walkies. Then he wanted to sit on my lap, which made typing virtually impossible, because every time he dozed off his nose hit the delete button on the keyboard, sending my unsaved work spinning into the electronic ether.

Most distracting of all was George's incessant barking. He stood beside my desk for hours on end, yelping with mind-numbing regularity. He barked and barked and barked. Why? Because he was hungry. Not hungry enough to eat the healthy dry rubble in his bowl, but hungry enough to make my life impossible. His food was turning into a full-scale battle of wills.

When I could stand no more barking, I carried George up to the kitchen and plonked him down in front of his untouched bowl of pellets. His face, which had looked happy for a few seconds, crumpled into an expression of abject misery, and the light of hope that had blazed momentarily in his cyes went out. Is this hard gravel *all* I'm going to be fed? he seemed to say. I knelt on the floor and tried to hand-feed him. Occasionally he crunched up a pellet or two joylessly, but for the most part he simply turned away his head.

After a fortnight on dry rations George grew lethargic and miserable. His face looked thin, and when I stroked him I could feel his ribs sticking out. I felt a failure as a mother — I mean, dog owner. I took him back to see Greg the vet.

"Why won't he eat anything?" I demanded, as I lifted the bundle of bones that George had become onto the examination bench, where he weighed in at only 4.5 kilos. "What am I doing wrong?"

Greg was young and disturbingly handsome, with large blue eyes and curly brown hair. He smiled at me reassuringly and, I hoped, flirtatiously. "I doubt you're doing anything wrong."

"When I put his food down, he looks unhappy, I'd almost say disturbed. Might he be ill, do you think?"

"Well, I've examined him, and from what I can see he seems to have no symptoms, other than lack of appetite."

"I know but . . . Could he be depressed because we've taken him away from his family?"

"Depressed?" he echoed, as George's wagging tail knocked over a bottle of disinfectant and sent it flying.

"Do you think he might be . . . ?" My voice petered out. I was unable to put my worst fear into words.

"Yes?"

I took a deep breath and came straight out with it. "Do you think he suffers from anorexia nervosa?"

Greg's mouth twitched. "In my experience it's unknown for a dog to deliberately starve itself," he assured me, struggling to keep a straight face. "George is probably just being fussy, as Cavs often are. He's probably balking at eating the all-in-one dry dog food and trying to manipulate you into giving him something else. But sometimes one has to be cruel to be kind, you know. I'd persist with the all-in-one, which really will be better for him in the long run. Look, if there's no improvement during the next few weeks, bring him back and we'll take a full medical profile of him, maybe do some bile tests."

"Great!"

"Perhaps you could try him on another flavor of the dry food in the meantime — lamb, for instance. Actually, I've got a few samples here." He tore open a packet and offered George a morsel. My dog wolfed it down so fast I thought he'd choke. "There, now. This stuff may well be the answer to your problems!"

I purchased a bag of the new food — at £13.60 ($26.98) a bag, it happened to be the most expensive flavor — and lugged it home. But, of course, when it was in his bowl George refused even to look at it. Instead, risking death and mutilation, he attempted to steal Monster Mog's tinned food from under her nose. The situation grew worse. Every time I roasted a chicken, George went hysterical with anticipation and yelped frantically when Joshua and I sat down to eat it. We learned at firsthand where the expression "barking mad" had originated. Whenever we reached a breaking point we surreptitiously slipped George the occasional chunk of chicken from our plates. One morsel followed another. And another. And another. But on the whole I held firm: I, not George, would win the food battle. If Greg insisted that premium-grade, all-in-one dry dog food was best for our Cavalier, that was what he would eat.

A fortnight on, there was still no improvement in George's appetite. I took him back to see Greg yet again and insisted that he do something about it. I left George at the practice overnight while he was tested for this and tested for that. Not only did the results all come out normal, George ate whatever he was given while he was in their custody.

"I wonder . . . Have you been feeding him scraps from the table?" Greg asked, when I went to pick George up and pay the bill (£157.32, or $312.11, including the overnight stay — I might as well have booked him into a four-star hotel).

"Hardly ever!" I insisted.

"Well, even though George is still very thin, he has put on a little weight, you know — point four of a kilo, actually." He narrowed his eyes, like a detective sussing out a criminal. "He must be eating something."

"I can't imagine what."

"Perhaps, to set your mind at rest, you should bring him in to be weighed every week from now on so that the nurses can monitor his progress."

Convinced that my poor dog was suffering from an eating disorder, I diligently took George for weekly weigh-ins. For the first time I was glad that Udi wasn't around to share an experience with me: he'd have had a field day. He'd always said I was a neurotic mother who worried unnecessarily over Joshua's health and diet. This was rubbish, of course. I was absolutely normal. If Joshua had a slight temperature, I assumed, like all mothers, that he was incubating some life-threatening disease and telephoned the doctor, no matter what time of night it was. And if he had a cold I kept him in, plastered his chest with layers of Vicks, and filled his room with menthol vaporizers. When he rejected my homemade organic spinach and fish pie or apple crumble in favor of frozen pizza and Maryland Cookies, I fretted about his salt consumption, his fat consumption, his sugar consumption, and the lack of vitamins, minerals, protein, and fiber in his diet. This time it was my dog's dinner that was driving me crazy with worry. And instead of getting better, the situation suddenly grew worse.

One day, about four months after he'd come to live with us, George stopped eating altogether. Abandoning the detested all-in-one dry dog food, I offered him tinned Whiskas, homemade scrambled eggs, and chopped-up organic roast chicken breast, but he wouldn't touch anything, even though I sat on the floor with him for hours trying to hand-feed him. Poor George just lay around listlessly, sapped of his normal joy and energy. Then he started throwing up — on the carpets, on the sofas, and for good measure, on my bed. My God, I thought, he's not just anorexic, he's bulimic as well! Large lumps of some vivid yellow substance speckled his Technicolor vomit.

"Mum?" said Joshua, coming upstairs to find me on my hands and knees, clearing up a pool of it. "Do you know where my ball's gone? The yellow foam one?"

We picked George up, jumped into the car, and drove straight to the vet's — a journey with which my car was already so familiar it could practically drive itself there. Showing only slightly more life than a slab of meat on a butcher's block, our precious Cavalier lay on the examination table while Greg gently prodded and poked him and Joshua and I stood by in tears. When he was taken away and X-rayed, George's guts were found to be full of a fuzzy, foam-like substance. Rather than operate immediately, Greg advised me to keep him under close observation and bring him back the following day.

Joshua and I spent the whole night keeping vigil over George. Monster Mog sat up with us, purring contentedly. To her chagrin, by morning her rival was almost back to normal, and after taking two more scans of his intestines, Greg decided there was no need for surgery. Even without it, the bill for the X-ray and two consultations was £120 ($238). The remainder of the yellow ball reappeared, free of charge, twenty-four hours later on the zebra crossing in the middle of Hampstead High Street. I'll spare you the full details.

George had illustrated in the most graphic way that he'd rather eat anything than all-in-one dry dog food. In my heart of hearts I didn't blame him — I wouldn't have wanted to eat it either. Rather than waste the huge sack I'd bought, I sprinkled the pellets over the lawn, expecting that the birds would swoop down and feast on them. They didn't. Neither did the local foxes. Instead, they lay scattered on the grass for a couple of weeks like tiny brown pebbles, then either rotted away or sank into the ground.

As with sleeping on the beds and sitting on the sofas, George had won the battle of wills again. Even Greg was beaten: after the foam-ball incident he prescribed a temporary diet of invalid-dog food (£2 — $4 — a tin), which my Cavalier wolfed with relish. After that, I put him back on roast chicken, followed by more roast chicken, and to add variety, roast chicken mixed with Monster Mog's Whiskas — when the cat wasn't looking.

NINE

In March 1999, my sister decided to introduce me to a man she'd met. She knew I was at a very low ebb, as was Joshua. Nine months after Udi's death, it had finally sunk in, in both our minds, that he was never coming back, and although George and his antics lightened our gloom much of the time, he couldn't of course dispel it.

Everyone in the family was living in the shadow of the double death that had afflicted us the previous June, and naturally my young son was affected most of all. Insecure and dreadfully sad, he was growing needier and more demanding by the day, and I wasn't doing a brilliant job of managing him. I tried to rise above his moods in order to keep our lives on some sort of even keel, but inevitably I got sucked into the vortex with him. Small arguments over everyday matters — what we should eat for supper or what time he should go to bed — quickly escalated into full-scale quarrels, and there was no third party to mediate or lay down the law.

Sue, my mother, and Tabby and Hannah were as supportive of us as they could be, but ultimately what happened next was down to me. Somehow I had to keep Joshua on track, and keep body and soul together by getting back to work. I knew, too, that we had to move on and create a new life for ourselves without Udi's powerful presence. But these things were easier said than done.

Anthony, Sue's friend, was a successful architect in his early sixties. He was also a widower: his beautiful young wife had died of breast cancer eight years before. Maybe it was the common bond of having lost our partners that drew us together, because, defying all my expectations, he and I hit it off instantly. I thought he was fantastic, and I think he must have liked me a little, because my domestic package didn't send him screaming for the nearest exit, although he didn't like dogs and absolutely hated cats.

As he recounted during the dinner party Sue gave to throw us together, his late wife, Jackie, had had three cats, Dinsdale, Ginger, and Norman. Anthony didn't particularly like any of them, but Norman, who was a female despite her name, really got to him. Though very small, she was completely fearless and rather vicious. Whenever she encountered the huge Great Dane that lived in the flat below them, Norman flew at him like a rocket, landing on his back and piercing his skin with her claws.

One day when Jackie was at work, their daughters were at school, and Anthony was working at home, the cats started jumping over his drawing board. "All three of the bastards," he told us over dinner. "Suddenly it was too much for me." Acting on autopilot, he stuffed Norman into a cardboard box, put the box into the car, and drove from their home in Camden Town to Hampstead. Then he walked to the most remote and wooded corner of the Heath, opened the box, let Norman out and walked away, leaving her there. He drove home without her. Even at the time he knew he was doing a terrible thing, but somehow he couldn't stop himself.

That night Jackie, with daughters Lara and Alice, went into the garden and called the cats in for dinner as usual. Dinsdale and Ginger turned up, but Norman didn't. Had Anthony seen her? they asked. No, he said, he hadn't. The following day the ritual was repeated, and the day after that, but Norman still didn't show. The girls scoured the local streets for their lost cat, and Jackie telephoned the animal rescue center to see if they had her. No luck.

Anthony watched all this from the sidelines, feeling thoroughly guilty. But by now it was too late to do anything about it. He thought he'd seen the last of Norman. Then, about six weeks later, he returned home from work one night to find Alice and Lara celebrating. "Guess what? Norman's turned up!" they cried exultantly.

Anthony walked into the kitchen. There was his nemesis, sitting on the table, thinner, filthier, mangier, and more flea-bitten than ever. She gave Anthony an accusing look, but he knew his secret was safe with her.

Anthony now realized that dumping Norman on Hampstead Heath had been shocking, but the way he told the story was so hilarious that even an animal lover like me had to fall about laughing. Only my brother-in-law, Philip, failed to see the funny side of it. I'm not sure if he ever quite forgave Anthony.

Some people might have thought that nine months after losing your husband was far too soon to start a new relationship. To me it was a blessing, almost a miracle. After years of being on my own, or in on-off relationships that had always led to disaster, I'd adored the thirteen years I'd shared with Udi — the ordinary, everyday domesticity as well as the more exciting parts. The last thing I'd wanted was to be on my own again, but fate had decreed otherwise, and I'd had no choice in the matter.

I hadn't expected to fall in love again, let alone so soon after Udi's death, but now I had. Anthony breezed into my life like a breath of spring air. He was talented, he was warm, he was witty, and he had the knack of reducing me to giggles. He loved good food and the cinema, and he was as handsome and rugged as any Mills and Boon hero. Not only was he stylish (his wardrobe was stocked with immaculate Prada sweaters and Armani jackets), he was also a fitness freak who lifted weights, went running every morning, and was a rugby maniac. What woman could have resisted him?

More important, because Anthony had been through a similar experience to mine, he understood instinctively much of what I was going through without having to be told. And, eight years down the line from his wife's death, he showed me that life didn't necessarily grind to a halt when one lost a partner. Another world existed on the other side of grief. And — dare one say it? — it could be exciting.

Anthony was terrific. I also took to his four charming and intelligent grown-up daughters — Lara and Alice by his late wife, Cindy and Justine from a previous marriage. But if I had any fantasies about us all playing happy families together, they were short-lived. Because Joshua loathed him.

Even at the time I knew that this was predictable. Nine months was far too soon for my son to contemplate allowing another man onto the scene. Who was this big muscular stranger who came into his house once a week? Would he try to take the place of Joshua's father? Would he come between us? Would he move in with us, start telling him what to do? In reality, none of these things was in the cards, but Joshua had no way of knowing it. All he knew was that he'd just lost his father and that now he was afraid of losing me, too. I tried to reassure him that I loved him more than anyone on earth, and that I would always put him first, but my words counted for nothing.

Since he was blessed with an optimistic nature, Anthony presumed that winning Joshua over would be possible, if not easy. One evening, he brought a troop of miniature mechanical robots to the house and spent two hours playing with Joshua at the kitchen table and explaining how the robots worked. For a short moment Joshua's icy front seemed to thaw a little, but afterward he immediately froze again. Several months later, when Anthony took him to his architectural practice and showed him the workshop where skilled craftsmen made miniature scale models of the ultra-cool minimalist buildings he designed, Joshua looked on in scornful silence.

Overly sensitive, perhaps, to Joshua's feelings, Anthony and I were careful not to appear too close in his presence. If I was so much as holding his hand in the kitchen, I'd drop it like a hot coal if we heard Joshua's footsteps thumping angrily upstairs in our direction, and if we were sitting side by side on the sofa, we'd spring apart like two north magnets as my son burst suspiciously into the living room. None of this helped the awkwardness of the situation. Whenever Anthony came over, Joshua prowled around the house like Hamlet, Prince of Denmark, at Elsinore Castle. We could almost hear him declaring, "Frailty, thy name is woman!"

Poor Anthony! He'd come round to see me after a hard day's work, hoping for a romantic evening. Instead, he'd find himself sitting two feet apart from me on the sofa, with George curled up between us, Monster Mog sitting on the armrest next to him clawing the upholstery with her talons, and the Moral Police (aka Joshua) patrolling the room to make sure that he and I didn't have any physical contact. That he stayed the course was something of a miracle.

Poor Joshua! His father's death had left him grief-stricken, and now he was angry, frightened, and confused. He could see that life was beginning to get a little better, but only for me, not him. Therein lay the awful, built-in inequality in our situations: I, his mother, could form a new relationship, maybe even find a new long-term partner, but he could never have a new father. When Udi died, he'd lost the irreplaceable. And that made me feel terribly guilty.

I contemplated ending the relationship for Joshua's sake, but something told me not to. Was I being selfish? Perhaps I was. I had no doubt that my son was my main priority, the very focus of my existence, but I also knew that I needed some kind of life outside the house if I was to survive the next few years without going crazy. Losing Udi and my father in the space of two weeks had taught me that life was far too precarious and short to waste. I had to grab what happiness I could, for Joshua's sake as well as my own. I'd be no good to him if I was miserable. Besides, I reasoned, Anthony was a busy man who enjoyed his independence. As far as I could see, there was no question of us moving in together, and as he didn't come to our house very much, Joshua only had to put up with him now and then.

But all the self-justification in the world counted for nothing when I looked at Joshua's long face. Worried that he was depressed, and that I was losing control of the situation, I hauled him off to see a family therapist. This brilliant man gave me what was probably the best advice any parent can hear: "Don't engage in useless arguments. And remember, he's the child in the relationship and you're the adult. You have to take charge. He needs you to."

From then on, instead of sitting opposite Joshua when we ate our meals together, I moved into Udi's place at the head of the table. Small as this gesture was, it helped me to exert some kind of parental authority. And instead of asking Joshua's advice on every family decision, I made up my mind what I would do and then told him what was going to happen. Joshua kicked up a storm at first, but he soon learned to accept that "No" meant "No" when I said it, and that there were times when arguing with me was useless.

As for Anthony, I hoped that Joshua would eventually grow to like him. But even after we'd been dating for six months, Joshua, at best, gave him the cold shoulder and, at worst, was actively hostile to him. Though Anthony was kindness and patience personified, Joshua continued to be rude to him, ignoring my demand that, though he didn't have to *like* Anthony, he *did* have to be polite to him. My newly acquired authority obviously wasn't that effective. Joshua still refused to say hello when Anthony came over. He interrupted him whenever he started to speak, and cut him dead if he tried to strike up a conversation. In fact, the only enthusiastic word Joshua ever said to Anthony was "Good-bye."

TEN

It was only natural that Joshua was upset by my new relationship. I'd expected him to act up, and he didn't disappoint me. What I hadn't expected was that George would act up, too.

Anthony was long-suffering about Joshua's attitude toward him. My pets were a different matter. I tried to persuade him that having animals around was a wonderful thing, but given his past experience with cats, it was a hard call. Monster Mog was her usual monstrous, vicious self — almost another Norman — and by the summer of 1999 George was well into canine adolescence. During May he spent a few days boarding with a Cavalier breeder while Joshua and I went away on a half-term break. He returned home a changed dog. A testosterone rush had kicked in, and the gleam in George's eyes had become more willful than teddy-bear sweet.

Since then he'd asserted his manliness around the house in the form of intermittent leg lifting, particularly in Joshua's bedroom. He bounded wildly across my bed, leaving trails of muddy footprints, and emptied every wastepaper basket in the house and chewed up the contents, leaving them strewn across the floor. He demanded to sit on my lap, even when I was working, and although I threw him out of the bedroom on nights when Anthony stayed over, he sometimes scrabbled at the door at three or four in the morning in a vain attempt to get back in.

Over the summer I came up with the idea that "family walks" on the Heath with George might soothe the growing friction between Joshua and Anthony, Anthony and George. How could I have been so stupid? Joshua dragged his heels and sulked, while George had developed an interest in chasing skirt. At the first whiff of a bitch, he strained at the leash, and the moment he was let off it, he bounded into the woods and wouldn't come back when we called him. "He's not like this usually," I assured Anthony, but he wasn't convinced. As the minutes ticked by and there was still no sign of George, Joshua grew increasingly distressed and angry, I grew tense, and

Anthony, understandably, became more than a little impatient. Shouldn't a dog be trained? he suggested tersely one night, as dusk was falling fast and George hadn't reappeared after half an hour.

Trained? Was formal dog training really necessary? Why, no one in my family had actually bothered to *train* a dog! In the 1950s my maternal grandparents, Laura and Phil, had owned a black cocker spaniel with the unimaginative name Blackie, who'd enjoyed the free run of Cricklewood, the North London suburb where we'd all lived. Though he was shut up in their house in Dicey Avenue when my grandmother left for work, Blackie invariably escaped and trailed her to the bus stop in Cricklewood Broadway, a distance of about a mile. En route, he was joined by most of the other dogs in the neighborhood, so by the time my smartly dressed, blue-rinsed grandmother reached the bus stop she was always leading a procession of a dozen or so barking mutts, rather like a canine version of the Pied Piper. When the bus arrived, Blackie insisted on jumping on it with her, abandoning his mates to the perils of the shops. But since her showroom in the West End, where she designed and made wedding dresses, was no place for a muddy, molting dog, she always put Blackie off at one of the stops before Kilburn and, in those relatively car-free days, left him to find his own way home, which he always did.

He'd often stop off at our house, a few streets from his own, to visit Gigi, our standard poodle bitch. Unlike the pedigree specimens you see at dog shows, all waxed legs and back-combed pom-poms in unexpected places, Gigi was covered with nose-to-tail tangles. Yet despite her untidy appearance she was undoubtedly the femme fatale of Cricklewood. Whenever she was confined at home in heat, a gang of randy mongrels gathered outside our house and kept up a chorus of off-key mating calls. If Gigi managed to get out, which she nearly always did (Blackie had obviously taught her a thing or two about escapology), she and her chosen playmate-of-the-month got down to business without a moment's hesitation, often on the driveway of our house, in full view of the neighbors.

"She's at it again!" my mother would shriek, when she spotted her through the window. Armed with a bucket of cold water, my father would go outside to put an immediate end to the fun and games. But he always arrived too late. A couple of months later, Gigi would give birth to a litter of odd-looking yet adorable puppies. It took weeks of frantic searching on my parents' part to find them all homes.

When I was eight, we moved from Cricklewood to a rambling mansion flat just north of Baker Street in London's West End. Unknown to my sister and me, Gigi was very ill. Since my adored grandfather had just died of lung cancer at the age of fifty-four, my parents were unwilling to break even more bad news to us, so they told us that, since it was unfair to keep a dog in a flat, Gigi was going to live at a farm on the Isle of Wight for her own good. The phrase "a farm on the Isle of Wight" will forever bring a chill to my heart for, as Sue and I found out when we were adults, there *was* no farm: it was a euphemism for euthanasia.

Though I had no inkling at the time of this heartbreaking fact, I was still inconsolable at losing my beloved dog and our small back garden. By sending Gigi away to live in the country and bringing me to live in an apartment in town, I sobbed, my parents were trying to kill me. Overcome with remorse — they'd just wanted to improve our lives by moving from the suburbs to central London — they disappeared to Harrods of Knightsbridge one afternoon where, in the store's pet-store-cum-zoo on the second floor, they purchased an eight-week-old Yorkshire terrier with their recently acquired account card. As she handed the squirming speck of tan, black, and gray fluff to them, the pet-shop-keeper said ominously, "Don't let him rule you!" My parents burst out laughing. The idea of the tiny, trembling bundle ruling anyone seemed ludicrous.

They should have taken note and handed it straight back to the pet-shop-keeper. Unaware that the speck of fluff was trembling with rage rather than fear, my parents wrapped it in my mother's coat and brought it home to Hanover Gate Mansions, where my sister and I instantly fell in love with it.

This was Freddy, whom my mother still missed some twenty years after his death. Though he was less than a foot high when fully grown, he dominated our lives for fifteen years. Though not the best example of his breed (his ears bent over in a rakish fashion, when they should have stood upright), in our eyes he couldn't have been more beautiful.

Although he pretended to be deaf when you called him to heel in the park, Freddy could hear a bar of Cadbury's Dairy Milk being unwrapped at a distance of fifty meters and was at your side within seconds, begging for a square. Always a fussy creature when it came to food, he eventually refused to eat anything except chocolate or boiled ox hearts, which had been recommended by the vet. Too embarrassed to admit that she was buying the hearts for her dog, my mother told our local butcher that my father had a penchant for them, but I'm not sure he believed her. "They're for *him,* aren't they?" he'd say, jutting an accusing finger across the counter at the snarling creature tucked under my mother's arm, and no amount of denial on my mother's part would persuade him otherwise. The pungent, sickly smell of stewing hearts pervaded my adolescence. Dissecting the huge, tough brown organs into little chunks — aorta, tricuspid valves, ventricles, congealed blood, and all — was a job my sister and I fought to avoid. As with all household chores, Sue somehow always succeeded in getting out of it. Had I not chosen to go to art college when I left school, I would have made a brilliant heart surgeon.

Having eaten so much heart, you'd have thought Freddy would grow sweet and loving. But he started off as a querulous puppy, and only became more so with time. What was he angry about? His home life was nothing to complain of, for he was adored and doted on by us all. Yet, like Monster Mog, he could never be trusted not to sink his sharp little teeth into whatever flesh was nearest.

Freddy snapped at other dogs and went for them regardless of their size. He barked crazily when visitors arrived at our flat, and became even more hysterical when they left. He particularly hated workmen — window cleaners, garbagemen, electricians, and anyone wearing a flat cap. The vet recommended that we try curbing Freddy's aggression by castrating him. He didn't take kindly to this — what male would? — and became more crotchety than ever.

If we hadn't all been so attached to Freddy, I'm sure he would have followed in Gigi's footsteps to that "farm on the Isle of Wight." But we loved him dearly despite his faults, and in Freddy's case love meant never having to say he was sorry. Even my father, who'd sworn at first he'd have nothing to do with looking after Freddy, developed a strong bond with him. In a household where his sex was outnumbered three to one, our Yorkie was Dad's only male ally. And after dealing with the ricocheting emotions of a wife and two stormy adolescent daughters, Freddy had a refreshing manly toughness that my father probably admired. Torn apart one night in the countryside by an equally angry Labrador he'd been taunting through a hedge, Freddy survived till the grand old age of fifteen, despite a heart condition and a chronic cough, both of which required expensive medication.

Was it possible to train a dog? I wondered. To my relief, George eventually reappeared and, smelling distinctly feral, was dragged reluctantly home, where he peed in Joshua's bedroom. It was certainly time to try. Since all the puppy-training classes in the area were fully booked, I telephoned a private dog trainer whom my next-door neighbor had recommended. Carol, too, had recently acquired a dog, a schnauzer named Snizz, and although Snizz wasn't exactly trained to military standards, she did at least come when called.

Enter Pete, and his little metal clicker. I'd have called him more of a dog therapist than a trainer. At £50 ($100) an hour, he certainly cost as much, and if his beard had been gray instead of black, he'd have been Freud's double. With his round tortoiseshell glasses and his corduroy jacket, patched at the elbows with leather, he looked every inch the old-fashioned academic or intellectual, and it was the intellectual approach he took with George.

While George lay on the couch, snoring gently, Pete and I sat down opposite each other at the kitchen table, and I told him the problem, or rather problems, I was having with my dog: incontinence, disobedience, willfulness, demolishing the garbage cans, his continuing abject fear of Monster Mog. While I spoke, Pete aahed, ummed, and nodded understandingly. So far I'd only spoken of my pets' shameful behavior to my mother and sister, who'd told me to pull myself together and tell them both off sharply when they were bad, so it was wonderful to get it all off my chest in front of someone who really understood.

"I just can't take it anymore!" I wept, wiping away the lone tear that had trickled down my cheek.

Pete waited for me to calm down. Then he said, "The first thing you should realize is that George's indoor puddles have absolutely nothing to do with bladder control. In my opinion he's seeking your attention."

"Right!" I said. But didn't George have enough of that already? I mean, I spent from dawn till dusk seven days a week looking after him. How much attention could one smallish dog need? Still, Pete was the expert, so I tried to keep an open mind.

"The fact that his favorite peeing place is in your son's bedroom speaks volumes about his intentions."

"Of course! Sure! Does it?"

"Clearly. Having failed to establish dominance over your cat, George is trying to establish his dominance over Joshua. His intention is obvious. He wishes to rule him."

As an armchair psychotherapist myself, I countered Pete's theory by suggesting one of my own:

"Do you think George might be missing the company of his own kind? You see, he *was* brought up as part of a large pack of Cavaliers until he was five months old. And suddenly, well, we took him away from them. Perhaps he resents us for it. I only say this because when we left him with another Cavalier breeder at half-term, he seemed perfectly happy. At least, he was incredibly happy when we picked him up." Actually, judging from his demeanor when we'd gone to collect him (gross indifference to us), George had had the time of his life.

Pete flashed me a patronizing smile. "You may have *thought* George was happy while boarding at the breeder's," he said. "He may even have *appeared* to be happy. But in all likelihood he was depressed."

What? Depressed while romping around

the fields near High Wycombe like an extra from *101 Cavalier King Charles Spaniels?* "Oh. Do you really think so?"

Pete nodded gravely. "He would have been missing the company of humans. Ask yourself how much individual attention he could have had there, with all those other dogs around."

I conceded that Pete might have a point. At home, George had the undivided attention of two humans for the best part of every twenty-four hours. We talked to him, we cuddled him, we rescued him from the jaws and claws of Monster Mog, and we threw balls for him in the vain hope he'd learn to run after them and bring them back to us. At the breeder's all he'd had was unlimited freedom and eighteen other dogs to play with — oh yes, and satellite television and Super Nintendo.

Pete shrugged off my next theory: that George was simply naughty. "You know," he said, "there's no such thing as a naughty dog. There are only misunderstood dogs. George is suffering from lack of self-esteem. What he needs at the moment is clearly a lot of positive reinforcement. Praise his good behavior. Ignore him when he's bad."

"Right. I see. But what should I do when he pees in Joshua's bedroom?"

"Ignore it. Say nothing. The worst thing you could do is to yell at him, or rub his nose in the wet patch. That would feed his desire for attention. I suggest that you clear the mess up only once he's left the room. On no account let him observe you doing it."

"Okay." I was fast losing faith in Pete, but then he got out a bag of dog treats and a little metal device that made a clicking sound. Using the treats as rewards, and the clicker as "an event marker to mark his desired response" (his words, not mine), he taught George to sit, come, and lie down to command, all in the space of a couple of minutes. This alone was worth the fifty quid. Fired with enthusiasm at the possibilities of training George, I had a go myself the moment Pete left the house.

"Sit, George!" I said, in my firmest voice, clicking the clicker.

To my delight, George sat, grinned at me, and wagged his tail.

It was time for some positive reinforcement: "Good boy! Clever boy!" I said, reaching for the treats. But before I could give him one, George leaped up, grabbed the packet, and ran out of the kitchen. By the time I caught up with him, the treats had disappeared down his gullet, the packet had been shredded, and there was a fresh wet patch beside Joshua's bed.

Feeling thoroughly inadequate, I telephoned George's breeder, Mrs. Colman, and asked her if I should really ignore George when he peed inside the house. She burst out laughing. The trainer had been talking nonsense, she said. A tap on the nose with a folded newspaper usually did the trick with her puppies, and to her knowledge, not a single one had grown up with emotional problems.

As for George's increasing wanderlust on the Heath, the vet said I ought to have him castrated before he ran under a car in pursuit of a bitch or disappeared for good. After a lot of soul-searching, and a few more tense walks with Joshua and Anthony, I drove my poor pooch to the practice one day and guiltily left him there while the dreadful deed was done.

ELEVEN

Christmas 1999 was the second we'd spent without Udi, and as on the previous occasion, I faced it with a heavy heart. In common with all parents, I wanted my child to enjoy a memorable holiday, which we celebrated in a secular way even though we were Jewish. But it wasn't going to be pain-free for either of us. No matter how we passed the days, or how much effort the rest of the family put into making it a great experience for Joshua, Christmas, as well as being a time to be thankful for what he'd just gained — by which I mean his presents — was inevitably a time when he'd mourn what he'd lost. Without his father, Christmas would never be the same.

It had always been a particularly special time of the year for Udi. Perhaps because his own childhood in postwar Austria had been one of deprivation and social ostracism, he threw himself into the festive spirit like an overgrown child. He'd shoot off on shopping expeditions to Soho, Hamleys, and Heal's on his motorbike, which, by the time it cruised slowly back to Hampstead, would have dozens of carrier bags dangling from the handlebars. There were silver bangles for Hannah, gizmos and toys for Nathaniel and Joshua, luxurious cosmetics and jars of her favorite pickles for Tabby, and, often, jewelry for me. Though it was a relatively small bike, large boxes containing electrical gadgets, such as a coffee machine, were sometimes strapped to the back, and, once, a wooden coffee table tied on with string.

Udi's Christmas trips to Heal's always included a visit to their decorations department, where he purchased the most extravagant and beautiful baubles he could find. Back home, he added these to the ones he'd collected over the years and laid them out on the sofa. Then, with Joshua perched precariously at the top of a stepladder, the two of them dressed our huge tree. A small, tasteful fir such as you saw in department store windows, simply adorned with monochrome bows, was not for Udi. His Christmas tree stood a brutish eight feet tall and was so bushy it took up almost half of the living room, and by the time he and Joshua had finished hanging everything on it, there wasn't a single naked branch. Between the opulent, garish baubles, the painted wooden trinkets, the old-fashioned candy sticks, the chocolate Father Christmases, and the fat, fluffy ropes of glittering tinsel were threaded three or four separate sets of flashing lights, at least one of which was musical. One set we had, made in China, played fourteen tunes, including, perplexingly, the socialist anthem otherwise known as "The Red Flag" — or so I presumed it was until Udi informed me that it was also the melody of a traditional German song called "O Tannenbaum," or "O Christmas Tree" and was used in the USA by Iowa, Maryland, Michigan, and New Jersey as the tune for their state songs.

There were real candles on our tree, too. Udi insisted on this. Fixed with special tin candle clips and inspired by the trees in his native Austria, where at least three or four homes went up in flames every year because of them, they remained unlit until Christmas Eve. Then, with me standing by clutching our Personal Kitchen Fire Extinguisher (the only potentially useful item we ever purchased from Innovations, apart from the mousetrap), Udi turned off all the other lights in the room and lit the wicks. Flickering in the darkness, the tree looked utterly beautiful. We stood around admiring it for five minutes or so and then snuffed out the candles. It was quite safe. Or so we thought.

One New Year's Eve, we threw a large party for family and friends. Our open-plan room was packed with small children, teenagers, and adults having a great time. Udi, who, despite his gusto for life, rarely drank much, had a glass or two too many that night and decided to light one of the candles on the tree. "Stop being such a neurotic!" he said when I protested that this was dangerous when we had so many people in the house. "I'm standing right here keeping an eye on it!"

And so he was — until his bleary eyes wandered to the desserts laid out on the kitchen table and he walked away absent-mindedly to help himself to a spoonful of chocolate mousse. Shortly afterward four-year-old Jessica came running up to me and said excitedly, "Auntie, the tree's on fire!"

I laughed at her sweet turn of phrase. "No, darling, it's just covered in electric ligh— Oh my GOD!" The candle had caught the branch above it, and little flames were running up it like an army of red and yellow ants. The entire tinder-dry Christmas tree, which was bristling with live electric cables,

163

was about to go up like a torch. Screaming for everyone to get back, I grabbed two cushions from the sofa and banged them together over the burning branch in an attempt to put out the fire myself. My instinctive action had the opposite effect of increasing its oxygen supply and causing it to spread. No wonder I'd been thrown out of the Brownies.

Seconds later Udi ran up with our Personal Kitchen Fire Extinguisher, only to discover that he hadn't a clue how to work it. Neither had I. Nor could either of us read the instructions printed on the side because the lettering was too small and we didn't have time to find our glasses. As the tree trunk caught, our friend Nigel came to the rescue and heroically beat out the flames with his bare hands, felling the tree in the process.

"How could you have been so stupid?" I screamed at Udi, as we flung open the windows to let out the smoke, and surveyed the smashed baubles, the scattered pine needles, the scorched cushions, and our blackened white walls. "You could have killed everyone!"

"But I'm sure I blew out the candle!" he protested lamely. Although he had the grace to look shamefaced for about five minutes,

Udi was soon laughing, and dined out on the story for ages afterward.

When Joshua woke up on Christmas Day, usually at some unearthly hour such as five a.m., he always brought his stocking into our bedroom and dumped out its contents while sitting on our bed. Meanwhile his TV producer father videoed him with the same professional care he would have taken if he was making a documentary for Channel 4. Seldom without a camera in his hand, Udi filmed practically everything Joshua did from the day he was born, including having tantrums, eating his meals, and building dens in the living room. Immediately afterward, he'd replay the images on television, while Joshua sat on his lap, either giggling or cringing at his antics. I often protested that watching an action-replay of his life on a television screen just minutes after he'd lived it might have a long-term detrimental effect on a young child, but Udi said that was nonsense, and as usual, he turned out to be right.

Every year Sue and I took turns to make Christmas lunch for our extended family, which usually numbered between twelve and fourteen people. Then, on Boxing Day, Udi, Joshua, and I were joined by Hannah, Tabby, her partner Carlton, and, eventually, their son Nathaniel, for a second family Christmas. Since the girls had already had a proper Christmas lunch with their mother the day before, food was less important than our annual Boxing Day walk. Donning Wellington boots, coats, and scarves, we'd all head for the Heath.

"Got your keys?" Udi asked me one Boxing Day just after he'd slammed the front door of our flat *and* the front door of the house behind us.

"No," I answered. "Haven't you got yours?"

There wasn't a locksmith to be found in North London on the 26th of December, so we called 999 and threw ourselves on the mercy of the Fire Brigade. Since they weren't busy that afternoon (luckily, the Austrian penchant for setting fire to one's Christmas tree hadn't spread to the general population of England), two huge fire engines rolled up outside our house and about a dozen burly firefighters jumped out. Joshua was thrilled, Udi less so, particularly when, after walking round the house and peering through the windows, they announced that we had so many locks and security devices that they were unable to break in without destroying the front door.

"This is your fault!" Udi snapped at me

as we all stood shivering out in the cold.

"*Mine?* Why?"

"If you hadn't insisted on turning the place into Fort Knox we wouldn't be in this situation!"

"We wouldn't be in this situation," I snapped back, "if *you* hadn't locked us out!"

Our subsequent blazing row, and the twin challenges of getting in while creating the minimum of damage and impressing my two beautiful stepdaughters in the process, spurred the firefighters on to bore through one of the ground-floor window frames with a drill, thus taking out its security lock. They were magnificent.

What could live up to the memory of such dramatic, fun-packed Christmases past? Now, like all the other bereaved people, for whom I'd never spared a thought before Udi died, Joshua and I ran the gauntlet of happy family images as the Christmas holiday approached. Smiling fathers opened presents on every advertising billboard, and smiling fathers carved the turkey on every TV commercial, and smiling fathers featured in the Christmas family films, which all seemed to end with a boy and his father being reunited after some long separation. The latter upset me most of all, and as an actor ran toward his film son, arms out-stretched, I'd make a dash for the bathroom so that Joshua didn't see me crying.

At those times I thought of my own father, too. It was normal to lose a parent when you were an adult, so during the past year and a half I'd sometimes run into a contemporary who'd recently lost his. Somewhat apologetically, given my own double loss, this person would tell me how shattered he felt, even if it hadn't been unexpected. Outwardly I sympathized, but inside a rather atrophied part of me wanted to tell my contemporary to pull himself together. I'd been so preoccupied with helping Joshua over losing *his* father that I'd scarcely had a chance to think about losing my own.

When I went out to do my Christmas shopping, I avoided the men's clothing departments as if they were infected with the Ebola virus, but in the unavoidable stationery departments the cards that inevitably caught my eye were those bearing the message "Happy Christmas, Dad." Though I'd never been particularly good at choosing presents for my father or Udi, I now spotted scores of items that I knew they'd have loved. I compensated by splurging on expensive gifts for Joshua. As I handed over my worn-out credit card, I told myself that

Christmas definitely wasn't a time to economize.

When was? I had to think seriously about saving money, because as the millennium approached I was fast running out of it. By now I'd plundered the small cushion of capital that Udi had left me, and my hopeless financial head was about to hit stony ground. Until Udi had fallen ill, I'd been trying to establish myself as an author of lighthearted so-called chick-lit novels, and since his death I'd made several stabs at starting a new one, but after two or three chapters I always ran out of steam and gave up. The trouble was I didn't feel lighthearted. Nor was I much of a chick now — in the latter half of my forties, I was more an old hen. During the last twelve months I'd earned scarcely anything except a few royalties, which always seemed to arrive just when I needed them most.

Perhaps now was the time to change careers and get a "proper job," as my parents used to call it. As an art school dropout who, despite my literary career, could barely type, couldn't spell properly or add, I was hardly God's gift to potential employers, but someone might want me. If they didn't, I told myself, I could always sell my possessions — if I had any worth selling. If I was really desperate, I quipped to my sister, I could even sell myself. Actually, I'd once jokingly suggested this to Udi at a time when we'd been strapped for cash. "Darling," he'd said in all seriousness, "I'm afraid you wouldn't make much money. You'd forever be telling the customers, 'No, sorry, I don't do *that*. No, nor *that*. And I certainly won't do *that* either!' "

When I announced that I'd be looking for a job in the new year, Joshua came up with a suggestion: "Why don't you become a dog walker, Mum?"

"A dog walker?" I looked at him as if he were mad.

"Think about it. You take George to the Heath every day anyway, so you might as well take other dogs at the same time and earn some cash."

"But, darling," I protested, "I need proper money. Dog walkers must earn peanuts."

"No, they don't. I asked one the other day, and she says she gets ten pounds every time she takes a dog for a walk. Look, if you walked ten dogs twice a day five days a week, say, and charged their owners ten pounds a time, that would be — hold on . . ." He totted it up on his fingers. "A thousand pounds a week!"

My jaw dropped — as much at my ten-year-old son's hitherto hidden business acumen as at the enormity of the sum, which I double-checked on a calculator. Joshua was right: by his calculations I'd make fifty-two thousand a year as a successful dog walker, at least double what I'd ever earned as a writer.

I pulled a piece of paper out of one of his homework books and scribbled down the pros and cons of becoming a dog walker. *For:* double my income; self-employed; would fit in with school holidays; could take George with me; joys of nature, etc.; plus endless exercise, which would mean an end to cellulite. *Against:* driving around North London in a smelly, flea-infested van, braving traffic wardens and car clampers while I stopped to collect charged-up canines from their luxury pads; striding across the Heath in the pouring rain in a mud-spattered anorak, shouting, "Molly! William! Rupert! Megan! Sebastian!" (we're talking posh North London dogs here); and, horror of horrors, picking up the dog shit that the aforementioned pedigree pooches would deposit on the ground.

The last one killed the idea for me. Picking up a strange dog's excrement must be even worse than changing the nappy of someone else's baby: you can just about cope with doing it for your own, but when it comes to someone else's, it's that much more gag-inducing. No, I'd have to find some other means of making money. If push came to shove, I had a fallback position, but I was reluctant to take it. As well-meaning advisers didn't tire of telling me, I was sitting on my best asset, and it wasn't my derriere.

In the months following Udi's death I'd consulted a professional financial adviser. "Your property is your most valuable possession," he'd told me. "What you should do is sell it, downsize, and let me invest the profit for you so that you can maximize your income. I mean, what do you need a three-bedroom apartment for, now that there are only two of you?" He was probably right, but I could have killed him for his insensitivity. This was Joshua's and my home he was talking about. Eighteen months on, it was also a continuing link to Udi, with whom I had created it and who had loved it. Everything, from the towel rails in the bathroom to the garden shed, had his stamp on it.

Traces of Udi remained in every cupboard and drawer in the form of old mobile phones, dusty notebooks with his handwriting in them, heavy bunches of mysterious keys he'd once carried around, and threads of pungent dark tobacco strewn at the bottom of the toolbox. Most poignant of all was Udi's Psion organizer, a now obsolete bit of technology that, weirdly, had cut out and died shortly after he had, taking with it to electronic heaven the last irreplaceable weeks of the diary he'd been writing ever since Joshua's birth.

Why was I still keeping these useless objects? There was no real answer to that question. Getting rid of them seemed too final for me. I'd only recently summoned up the courage to go through Udi's wardrobe and deal with his clothes. Gritting my teeth one afternoon when Joshua was out of the house, I'd bagged everything up, loaded it into the car, and taken it to an Oxfam shop on the other side of London — any closer to home and I might have risked bumping into some stranger dressed as my late husband's ghost. As for Udi's shoes, I hadn't been able to stomach the thought of anyone else putting their feet inside them so I'd thrown them away — except one rather eccentric black pair with straps and buckles that he'd worn on our first date. These I'd stashed at the back of my own wardrobe, alongside Udi's secondhand coat with the fur collar, a couple of jackets that reminded me of him, and his favorite black velvet shirt.

As the twenty-first century approached, I knew it was time to let go of these things, perhaps even of the flat, and move on a little further. But that was easier said than done. Where was I going? My relationship with Anthony was foundering. Joshua's attitude was not the only thing to have come between us: we'd met at the wrong time — too soon after Udi's death, perhaps, and also at very different stages of our lives. I was looking for someone with whom I could have a second stab at domestic bliss, a man who was willing to take on my son as well as me. The older Joshua got, the more I realized how much he needed a strong male presence in his life, and I was desperate to provide one for him. In many ways Anthony would have made a perfect stepfather, but Joshua couldn't see it.

Neither, to be honest, could Anthony. He'd really tried with Joshua, but when he'd seen that he was getting nowhere, he'd understandably given up. And, in his heart of hearts, he didn't really want to be tied down to a woman with a young child: he'd already been there and bought the T-shirt twice. His youngest daughter, Alice, was now an adult, like her three older sisters, and for the first time since his early twenties Anthony was able to enjoy a relatively carefree existence. It included going out most nights, taking frequent holidays, and at weekends watching hours of uninterrupted sport. The idea of taking on board not just me but George, Monster Mog, and Joshua — "the whole domestic caboodle" as he called it — was too much for him. And who could blame him?

As I was discovering, it was hard to negotiate the logistics of a new relationship when your first priority was your child. For starters, spontaneity went out of the window. You couldn't go out to the cinema at short notice, or stay overnight at your boyfriend's house, or be away for more than a few hours without making elaborate arrangements. Romantic weekends were the stuff of dreams. Planning two nights in Paris with Anthony that autumn had been as complicated as organizing the invasion of the Falklands, if without the ships and tanks. Joshua's every minute had to be accounted for, his movements charted, his whereabouts known at all times of day and night. Telephone numbers and house keys had to be circulated among my family and the parents of Joshua's friends, and a list of instructions for feeding Monster Mog given to a next-door neighbor. As for George, I ended up sending him to the Paw Seasons, a unique country hotel for dogs, which turned out to be far more luxurious and welcoming than the one Anthony and I stayed in on Paris's Left Bank.

This, by the by, was a disaster in its own right. After hours of research I'd found the hotel on the Internet. Delightfully traditional though the old house was, it was situated next to a set of traffic lights between the busy Boulevard St. Michel and the even busier Boulevard St. Germain, and our first-floor room had big French windows that weren't double glazed. We might as well have tried to get some shut-eye on the central reservation of a major freeway as in that picturesque brass bedstead. The vibration and sound of traffic zooming past, braking, or revving kept Anthony and me awake throughout the first night; it sounded so close at times that we feared we might be run over. Exhausted, and distinctly touchy with one another, we spent most of the following day tramping the nearby streets in search of a quieter location. After visiting practically every hotel in the *quartier,* only to discover they were all fully booked, we eventually found one with a vacant attic room, which had just one small window.

"Oh, isn't this wonderful?" we sighed, as we sank gratefully into bed that evening, hoping for nothing more romantic than to catch up on our sleep. Two minutes later the silence was broken by raised voices, loud rock music, laughter, and popping champagne corks. I jumped out of bed and twitched open the curtain. A wild Parisian party was going on in a loft across the street, and all the double glazing in France couldn't deaden the sound of it.

Paris had been the kiss of death for our relationship, which petered out soon after we returned. Although we remained on good terms, I was facing Christmas and New Year's on my own. My little Hamlet may have been happier without "Uncle Claudius" around, but I was so sunk in gloom that I couldn't face decorating the Christmas tree. On Christmas Eve Tabby, Hannah, and Nathaniel came round to help us do it, while George made his own contribution by shredding the scrunched-up newspaper in which the baubles had been wrapped. As I watched them all having fun together, it occurred to me that at least one wonderful thing had emerged from the aftermath of Udi's death: I'd been scared that I'd lose contact with my stepdaughters, but instead the opposite had happened and we drew ever closer.

That night, after they'd gone home, the flat seemed horribly empty again. "I wish Dad was here," Joshua confided, as we sat side by side on the sofa watching television with George stretched across our laps, his stomach bloated with the mince pies he'd found under the kitchen table that afternoon.

"So do I, darling," I answered. "So do I." We burst into tears. But grief had by now become a fast roller coaster, and fifteen minutes later we were laughing out loud together.

As I lay in bed later that night, worrying about my finances and waiting for Joshua to fall asleep so that I could deliver his loaded stocking to his room — his disbelief in Santa had been suspended for the night — I found myself missing Udi terribly. Then I heard a clunk in the hall as George came in from the garden through the cat flap. A few seconds later his nose pushed open my bedroom door and, tail wagging, he marched in. Raising his head to ascertain Monster Mog's position (she was currently curled up by my feet), he jumped onto the bed, carefully avoiding her, and trampled across my knees leaving a trail of muddy paw prints in his wake.

"George! What are you *doing?* Get off!"

Ignoring my protests, he sat down heavily on my stomach, looked me straight in the eyes, and as if he sensed I was feeling low, set about licking off the hand cream I'd just rubbed in. Despite the mess he'd caused, I appreciated the loving gesture, and when I stroked his long, curly Cavalier ears, he lay down across me and fell asleep, with a deep, contented sigh. Suddenly I began to feel better. It was impossible to mope with George around.

As I tousled the tufts of hair that, since his castration, had started to grow upright in cartoon style on top of his head, my eyes focused on an old black-and-white engraving that hung on the wall opposite my bed. I'd bought it in 1989, when I'd been pregnant with Joshua and writing a history book about the Central London district of Soho. The engraving, which had been made in the eighteenth century, was of Soho Square, the smartest address in the then highly fashionable area. It had also been the home of an extraordinary woman who had never ceased to fascinate me. Her name was Teresa Cornelys.

Teresa's life story was amazing. The daughter of an actress and a theatrical impresario, she'd been born in 1723 in Venice, which was then the sex-tourism and party capital of Europe — a place just as wild as today's Ibiza, only infinitely more beautiful and sophisticated. A femme fatale from her teenage days onward, fifteen-year-old Teresa had captivated the heart of a seventy-five-year-old senator, who begged her to marry him. She'd also flirted with fifteen-year-old Giacomo Casanova; years later, her brief fling with the famous lover had culminated in the birth of their daughter, Sophia.

By her early twenties the extravagant Teresa had made a name for herself as a soprano and a high-class courtesan at the royal courts of central Europe. But by her mid-thirties she'd lost everything she'd earned and was virtually begging in the concert halls of Amsterdam. As she approached what was then middle age, her angelic singing voice was fading, as were her physical attractions, which had so far stood her in equally good stead. The usual fate of aging actresses and singers at that time was to become a prostitute. But Teresa's determined attitude, coupled with her amazing talent, ensured that the most colorful and successful period of her life had yet to begin.

In 1759 Teresa brought five-year-old

Sophia to live in England. Although she hadn't a penny, and didn't speak a word of English, she managed to enlist the help of some of the most aristocratic women in London, raid the funds of a wealthy English lover, and open a set of smart assembly rooms in Soho. Carlisle House, as her vast, beautifully decorated premises on the east side of Soho Square were called, was in effect the world's first nightclub and rave venue. It catered to the rich and the royal, the famous and the infamous, and to serious intellectuals as well as effete poseurs.

Within a matter of months the fabulous concerts, all-night balls, and glamorous masquerade parties Teresa gave at Carlisle House were gossiped about not only in London but in newspapers as far afield as the American colonies. Teresa became a celebrity and, very probably, the highest-earning businesswoman in England. Yet by the time of her death some forty years later she'd lost everything, including her precious daughter, and was forgotten by the society people who had once feted her.

I'd been obsessed by what little I knew of Teresa's life since I'd first discovered her name in an old book about Soho. I admired her feistiness and ruthlessness and, most of all, her indestructible spirit. Life had dealt her some harsh blows, including repeated bankruptcies, the breakup of her marriage, spells of imprisonment, and the death of at least one of her children. Yet time after time she'd picked herself up and started again, no matter what the odds were against her.

Since Udi's death, the indomitable Teresa had been something of an inspiration to me. When she'd arrived in England she'd had literally nothing, but that hadn't stopped her reinventing herself. Compared to her, what did I have to complain of? If she could rebuild her life from nothing but the ashes of her past failures, well, so could I rebuild mine.

I was always on the lookout for new information about Teresa, and I dreaded finding out that someone else was writing her life story before I got round to doing it; I knew I'd kick myself. "Why don't you stop talking about it, and get on with it?" Anthony had admonished me, rather impatiently, shortly before we split up, as I'd been droning on about Teresa yet again.

That Christmas Eve, as the bells for Midnight Mass tolled at one of the nearby churches, I gently pushed the sleeping George off my stomach, climbed out of bed, and examined the engraving of Soho Square more closely. There stood Teresa's house, on the right-hand side of the picture. Above it was Charles Street, which led straight upward, across what was then called the Tyburn Road and is today known as Oxford Street, to a little windmill at the edge of what was then countryside. I traced the path directly northward to a small hill at the top of the picture, beside which was written the word "Hampftead" in old-fashioned script — the place where I now lived. There was even a minuscule church drawn at the top, the same church whose bells I was now hearing.

A shiver passed down my spine. There, before my eyes, was a direct link between me and Teresa. In that moment I felt her calling to me across the centuries. Suddenly I knew that it was up to me, and me alone, to bring her to life again. Anthony's blunt words had shamed me at last into action. I'd give up trying to write a chick-lit novel and write Teresa's biography instead.

TWELVE

Immediately after Christmas, I wrote down the little I knew about Teresa's life and sent it to my literary agent. To my amazement, my outline for the biography was accepted by a publisher. I was back in business as a writer.

To be paid to piece together Teresa's story was like being given a marvelous present. There was a problem, though: who would look after Joshua while I was stuck in distant libraries researching the book? I didn't want him coming home from school to an empty house day after day, and neither did I want to leave him to his own devices for long stretches of time during the school holidays. My son was a strong character, and so far he'd weathered the loss of his father much better than I'd dared to hope. But these were early days. I knew from all the literature I'd read on the subject that fatherless boys were more than usually vulnerable to going off the rails, and I was determined that Joshua would have the most stable home life I could possibly provide.

There was also the added problem of what to do with George when I was working. I could hardly leave him home alone all the time either — or, rather, not alone but at the mercy of Monster Mog. Eighteen months after our Cavalier had joined the family, she was still waging war against him, and still clearly determined to win by any possible means. She'd treated George abysmally since the day he'd arrived, but since he'd been castrated her behavior toward him had become intolerable. Perhaps she sensed that he was no longer an "entire" dog, as the vet euphemistically put it, and so took even more advantage of him than she'd done before. The tactics she used against him changed from casual, sporadic violence into all-out attack. Slashing George's face, boxing his ears, stealing his food, hissing, scratching, pouncing on him when he least expected it — all of these were now everyday occurrences, carried out with increasing force.

"Growl at her, George! Go on, bark!" I urged him. But no matter what I said, George wouldn't or couldn't put up a fight. There had never been an ounce of aggression in his character even before his castration, and since the op he'd turned into a double-wuss. Unlike Charles I's followers, who might have lost the Civil War but had at least fought back against the Roundheads, our Cavalier was even incapable of self-defense.

The family volunteered to look after both Joshua and George as much as they could, but I could hardly rely on them all the time, for they were even busier than I was. As well as having young Nathaniel to look after, Tabby worked all hours of the day and night for a housing charity. Hannah, who'd once worked in the music business, was now retraining to become a nurse, a career she'd found herself drawn toward during Udi's illness. Sue was switching careers, too. In the past she'd been a freelance journalist specializing in writing about media, but now she was becoming a television and film producer herself. As for my mother, she'd recently returned to London from France, where she'd found life without my father intolerably lonely, and after more than twenty years abroad, she was readjusting to living in England.

Miraculously, an answer to my problem turned up when a Czech friend, Eva, told me that her twenty-year-old niece wanted to become an au pair in England for a few months and asked if I knew of a host family who might have her to live with them. I telephoned all my friends to ask if they would like some temporary help. Then it dawned on me that if anyone needed an au pair, I did.

Linda was a dream — attractive, clever, and vivacious. She spoke perfect English and was one of the most driven people I've ever met. Though her duties were only to look after Joshua and George for a few hours a day, she scrubbed the house from top to bottom, mowed the lawn, decimated the jungle of weeds that had taken over the flower beds, and cleaned out every drawer and cupboard, all without being asked. When I came home one evening and saw what she'd done to the mass of crumpled washing that had been crammed into the hamper, I cried. I'd never seen anything quite so beautiful as those neatly arranged piles of crisply ironed sheets, pillowcases, and towels: the place looked like a linen store. Linda was so efficient that she even found a replacement for herself before she returned to the Czech Republic at the end of the summer: she was the beautiful, doe-eyed Barbara, a friend of hers from back home who'd also come to England as an au pair, and had fled her host family when the husband made advances to her.

Linda and Barbara were the first of a handful of young Czechs who would share our home over the next four years. One lasted only a couple of days before parting company with us, but another, Martina, a tall, beautiful blond law graduate with a pin-sharp mind, ended up staying for two and a half years. During this time she fell under George's spell, endeared herself to everyone in the family, and amassed a collection of high-heeled shoes and boots that would have turned Imelda Marcos green. They spilled out of her tiny wardrobe in an avalanche of black leather and lay in great heaps all over the floor.

Martina and her compatriots not only took care of George's morning walk, baby-sat if I went out at night, and were there for Joshua when I wasn't at home during the day, they also generated a life of their own. I loved having them with us even though it meant that I was forced to write my book in a corner of my bedroom, as my study had had to be turned into a room for them. The house no longer felt too quiet or too big for us. In fact, it was quite the opposite: noisy and bustling, and we were packed in like sardines. The occupants now regularly embraced large gangs of Joshua's buddies and a host of visiting Czech friends and relatives. These included Barbara's mother, who, the minute she arrived to stay for a week, put on an apron and started making apple strudel in the kitchen, and Martina's best friend Ivona, another glamorous blond law graduate, whose au pair job in nearby Belsize Park entailed caring for her employer's epileptic beagle — he sometimes came to visit George.

With their respective canine charges perched on their laps, and looking as immaculate as if they'd stepped out of *Vogue,* Martina and Ivona were forever sitting around the kitchen table in full makeup, drinking homemade cappuccino and prattling away at top speed in their native tongue. "You'll never learn English if you carry on talking to each other in Czech," I warned them as they chatted away about God-knew-what — probably what they'd been up to the night before. Their social lives were to die for. Dressed like film stars, they went out clubbing at least twice a week, leaving the house at ten thirty or eleven p.m. and not coming home until four or five the next morning. Up at seven thirty to go to language school, Martina would spend the day looking fetchingly wrecked, but was never, ever in a bad mood. However tired she was, she always had a smile on her face, a soothing word to calm my hysterics, and the knack of finding my lost keys.

With Martina around to shoulder some of the domestic burdens and a new book to write, my life settled down into a routine for the first time since Udi had died. As I became less strained, Joshua grew happier. He and I were finally in a good place in our lives. Sadly the same couldn't be said for George. Though he, too, adored Martina, and sometimes trotted around the house in her wake in the same way that he shadowed me, the strain of living with the enemy — Monster Mog — took its toll on his health, and he became one of our vet's most regular patients. Over the next two years I took him to the vet's office more times than I care to remember. Okay, I do remember: it was an embarrassing forty-two times. His medical bills practically paid for the practice's new extension: they were thinking of calling it the George Wing. If it hadn't been for pet health insurance, I'd have been bankrupt, just like Teresa Cornelys.

George saw the vet about infected ears (four times, at an average cost of £60, or $120, a visit), a sore throat (twice, for £57, or $113), sore skin (countless times, bills astronomical, of which more later), and a small but odd-looking warty lump on his back that had to be removed under general anesthetic at a cost of £237.30 ($470.79). Since his teeth weren't being brushed properly (mea culpa) and his diet was less than perfect (ditto), his canine canines soon became encrusted with tartar and had to be descaled by a dental dog hygienist, also under general anesthetic, for £285.99 ($567.38). After this op George developed a cough and was put on antibiotics (£37.83, or $75.05). Then he caught fleas from Monster Mog, which meant they both had to be sprayed with insecticide, as did the entire house (time spent: six hours, bill £165, or $327, including a night in a hotel). Then George stepped on a piece of broken glass and cut the main pad of his left forefoot (a snip at £43.56, or $86.42). Since the wound was too small to be stitched (which would have meant another general anesthetic), I had to tie a plastic bag around it every time we went for a walk and bathe it twice daily in disinfectant.

No sooner had his paw pad healed, than George was pounced on by a boisterous Labrador. She meant no harm — she was just up for a bit of rough and tumble — but, sadly for both of them, our less-than-entire Cavalier was no longer interested in the opposite sex. In the ensuing one-sided tussle one of his claws was torn off, which meant yet another operation (and yet another bill, this one for £363.10, or $720.37). To stop him chewing his stitches, Greg put a large plastic cone rather like a lampshade around George's neck. While he was wearing this, he went foraging under my bed for old tissues and got stuck among the suitcases I stored there. As he wriggled his way out backward he slipped a disc. With his whimpers sounding in our ears, Joshua and I took him to an all-night veterinary hospital in Camden Town, where painkillers were administered and weeks of house arrest prescribed.

After George's first bout of gingivitis, I'd reinstated my ill-fated toothbrushing regime, but with no more success than the first time around. Martina took over, and fared a little better. Nevertheless George was soon back on the operating table for more dental descaling and the first of many tooth extractions. At the same time, he was given tests for the itchy skin patches and blackheads that were beginning to plague him. What with gum treatments, biopsies, laboratory tests, and medication, the bill that day came to an astronomical £930.98

($1847.00) — enough at the time to have bought three brand-new Cavalier puppies from Mrs. Colman.

And so it went on. Allergies, backache, conjunctivitis, diarrhea . . . The list of George's ailments soon read like an A–Z of canine complaints. I was so busy looking after him that I scarcely had time to work. When I wasn't at the wheel of my car driving him to or from the veterinary practice, I was on my knees at home, bathing him in special shampoos, squirting liquid painkillers down his throat, or wrapping bright pink pills in bits of cheese in order to trick him into swallowing them. However much Gouda, Cheddar, or Laughing Cow I molded around them, George always managed to eat the cheese and deposit the untouched pills on the floor.

I began to feel extremely responsible for George's frequent mishaps and illnesses. When I'd first had him, he'd been in perfect health, so perhaps everything that went wrong with him was my fault. Maybe I suffered from Munchausen syndrome by proxy, and I was deliberately making him ill without knowing it. But as Greg reassured me on the day we clocked up our fortieth visit (it was his itchy skin again, and the bill this time was £77, or $153, which included a small bag of antiallergy food and a bottle of antifungal shampoo), George simply seemed to be unlucky. Stuff happened to him.

And, in the spring of 2001, stuff started to happen all around the house.

THIRTEEN

Joshua was the first to discover it. He came home from school one afternoon and, as was his habit, grabbed the remote controls and threw himself down on the sofa in front of the TV. But instead of remaining in this couch potato position until bedtime, as was his wont, he immediately sprang up again.

"Ugh!" he cried. "The sofa's soaking wet!"

"What? Are you sure?" I said.

He gave me a withering look. "Mum, remember when I told you there was a bird flying around the living room and you didn't believe me?"

"How could I forget? It messed all over the carpet."

"Well, I was eight then and I'm eleven and a half now. Don't you think it's time that you started taking me seriously?"

Joshua was growing up faster than I cared to acknowledge. He was, I thanked my lucky stars, turning into a normal preteenager, by which I mean he was normally surly, normally slobby, and normally incomprehensible: a more accurate transcription of the above sentence would read, "Weh, ah-zate thenan arm levnarf nah. Donchafink stime usedarted taki mi seerslee?" I bit back my usual criticism of his pronunciation, if you could call it that, and inspected the sofa. There was indeed a large wet patch on one of the seat cushions. A single, brief sniff told me it was urine. An even briefer touch told me it was lukewarm and that whichever animal had committed this crime had done it recently. I swung round in search of a culprit. Both George and Monster Mog were right behind me.

"Which of you two did this?" I said. Neither owned up or pointed the finger of blame at the other. Blinking at me inscrutably, Monster Mog leaped onto the sofa. As she sniffed the offending cushion, her tiny nostrils flared with distaste. How revolting is *this?* her expression said, as she stepped up onto the sofa's arm, lay down facing us, and crossed her front paws with studied complacency.

I turned to the other potential culprit. Head cocked to one side, three-year-old George smiled up at me with large, moist, trusting eyes. He looked so friendly, so sweet, so kind, so wonderfully *good*. Surely he hadn't peed on the sofa. He'd been house-trained for ages, and besides, I'd taken him out less than an hour ago to water the pavement. I simply couldn't believe he was responsible, especially since the sofa was one of his favorite places to curl up.

I looked at Monster Mog again. She blinked at me with a serene, untroubled gaze. She certainly had her faults, but pee-ing indoors had never been one of them. I looked at George, and as I narrowed my eyes at him, he turned his face away and lowered his head. At the same time, his tail, which was pointing at the ground for once, flicked from side to side in small, furtive movements. "Did you do this?" I asked suspiciously, grabbing him by the collar, lift-ing his front paws onto the sofa, and point-ing his nose at the wet patch. After a quick sniff he wriggled out of my grip and backed away, looking guilty.

Like a sibling showing solidarity against a parent, Joshua jumped to George's defense. "Leave him alone! Remember what that dog trainer said? Ignore bad behavior and praise what's good! Besides, he might not have done it! And if he did, well, maybe he had an accident!"

That had to be the explanation. Anything

else didn't bear thinking about. In which case, there was no point in telling the poor dog off. Like a child who'd wet the bed in its sleep, George needed understanding, not chastisement. But unlike Joshua, who now picked him up and cuddled him, I wasn't in the mood to give it to him. Halfway through writing my book on Teresa Cornelys, I had plenty of work to do downstairs and could well do without clearing up his mess.

I snapped on a pair of rubber gloves, hauled the heavy seat cushion off the sofa, unzipped the loose cover and prized it off. I groaned. The huge, white, feather-filled cushion had a big yellow stain in the middle. It looked like a giant, soiled incontinence pad. How on earth was I going to clean it? "I guess we'd better wash it," I said to Joshua.

"Yes, Mum," my son agreed. "I guess *you* better had. Course, I'd love to help but I've got far too much homework."

"But you were just sitting down to watch television!"

"Yeah, but I've got to change, now, haven't I? I sat in the puddle, didn't I?"

"Thanks a lot."

My irony was lost on him. "You're welcome," he said, in a surprisingly polite manner, and ran downstairs.

"Joshua, come back and help me!" I called.

"I would, promise, only I can't hear you."

Wondering what kind of a monster I was bringing up, I carried the cushion to the bathroom, dumped it in the bath, turned on the hand shower, and started to scrub ineffectively at the stain. I hadn't a clue how I was going to get rid of the urine that had already soaked into the stuffing without washing the whole thing, and no idea how I'd ever dry it.

The main suspect trotted into the bathroom, put his paws up on the edge of the bath next to me, and kept me company by repeatedly pushing my scrubbing arm off course with the tip of his nose. George seemed to have got over his embarrassment remarkably quickly, for he was smiling again and the white flag of his tail was held high and wagging as usual. Over the last year I'd taught him to jump into the bath whenever we came home from Hampstead Heath, so that I could shower the mud off his paws. Presuming, I suppose, that this was what was expected of him now, he backed off, took a running jump at the bath, and leaped right in. "Get out!" I cried as he trampled over the cushion and dodged in and out of the spray. I dropped the showerhead, picked

George up, and set him back on the bathroom carpet. Meanwhile the shower hose swiveled round like a snake, spraying me and the walls.

Thoroughly enjoying this brilliant new game, George barked wildly and jumped back into the bath. I picked him up and deposited him on the floor again, shouting, "Stay!" at the top of my voice. Unlike him, I wasn't in the mood for games. At last he got the message. He shook himself hard, drenching me, then rolled on his back on the bathroom floor to dry himself, kicking his legs in the air. "Stop that!" I cried, grabbing his collar — but there was little point: the carpet was already soaking. So was I, and so, more importantly, was the sofa cushion, because I'd forgotten to turn the taps off while I was busy with George. Like a huge sponge, the feather stuffing had absorbed gallons of water.

It was now so heavy that it took all of my strength and Martina's to drag it out of the bath and deposit it on top of a hot radiator, where it remained, dripping steadily, until it dried out a week later. Despite my efforts to remove the yellow stain with a selection of industrial-strength chemicals, it didn't come out. Nor did the smell, even after I'd sprayed it with my best perfume.

When the loose cover eventually returned from the dry cleaner, order was restored to our messy living room. At last the sofa was back to normal, if a little whiffy. Then, two days later, as I was trying to get down to work in my bedroom, an apologetic Martina popped her head round the door.

"Judith, please come," she said. "Wet on sofa is happened for second time."

The phantom had been at it again. Once more the finger of blame pointed at George. This time I was furious. Forgetting Pete-the-dog-trainer's advice to ignore my dog's misdemeanors, I shouted at George, rubbed his face in the wet patch, and tapped him lightly on the behind with a rolled-up newspaper. With a bewildered and reproachful look at me, he scuttled away and hid under the kitchen table, his tail hanging pathetically between his legs. Monster Mog watched from the kitchen mantelpiece, smirking with an I-told-you-so expression. She'd always thought the dog was a filthy usurper who wasn't to be trusted, and now she'd been proved right.

From then on, George was taken out for a walk every hour on the hour. Nevertheless we soon discovered he'd done another puddle, this one on my bed. By the time I found it, the urine had soaked through the duvet and into the mattress. I yelled at him, yanked off the bedding, sprayed the mattress with disinfectant, and took the mattress cover to the launderette, and by the time I came back, George — for it was obviously him — had peed on the sofa again.

This was what my life had come to, I reflected as I hauled off the seat cushion, threw it back in the bath, and started scrubbing it again. It was the stuff of nightmares. There was nothing worse than urine soaking into a seat cushion or a mattress: no matter what lethal chemicals you applied to it, the smell never came out. By the end of that week, every bit of bedding we owned was stained, despite repeated boil-washing. Wet cushions were drying on every radiator, neither of the sofas had seats, and the entire house reeked like a concrete stairwell in a multistory car park.

I telephoned Pete, confessed all, and asked his advice. He ummed and aahed just as he had at my kitchen table: I could almost see him adjusting his Freudian-style spectacles and stroking his beard. "If you manage to catch George in the act," he said after a great deal of thought, "it might be worth telling him off very gently."

"And if I don't?"

"Well, in that case, chastising him would

be worse than useless. Counterproductive, even. To solve the problem, you need to go to the very root of it. If I were you, I'd look beyond George's puddles and into his soul."

"His soul? Right."

"Because, you know, by secretly urinating on the furniture George is obviously trying to communicate with you at a subliminal, very deep level."

Oh yes, obviously. The level at which George was trying to communicate was so deep that it had now penetrated not only the sofa cushions and cover, but also the frame. Pete suggested that I book a course of intensive canine therapy for him — ten sessions at £40 each ought to do it — but instead I hung up, ordered George to stay off the furniture in perpetuity, and casually dropped the words "Battersea" and "Dogs' Home" into my conversation. Hopefully, subliminal communication worked both ways.

Unfortunately George didn't get the message. Over the next seven days, as I became more annoyed with him, he grew more confused and anxious. At the same time, Monster Mog was more loving than she had been in years. Perhaps she had grasped that I was disillusioned with her deadly enemy, and was making the most of it. Since he was now relegated to the floor, she jumped onto my lap whenever she could and allowed me to stroke her without scratching or biting. Occasionally she even purred.

Poor George looked on in silent horror, as if he couldn't believe what was happening. My mother felt sorry for him. But, then, she didn't have to live with him. "Perhaps the poor little thing's ill," she suggested to me.

"Oh my God, Mum, perhaps you're right!" Feeling guilty, I hauled George off to see Greg the vet again. Looking more handsome than ever, he stuck a thermometer up George's bum, pressed his ribs, and listened to his heart. "There doesn't *seem* to be anything wrong with him," he announced. "However, it's possible he's picked up a bladder infection which is causing him to lose control of himself. To be on the safe side I'd like to test his urine."

"Sure. Whatever it takes."

"There will be a charge, of course. And I'm going to need your help."

"I'll do anything. Anything at all." He handed me a see-through plastic bag containing a little glass jar. "What's this?" I asked, trying to sound casual.

"It's a sterile specimen bottle. When George next lifts his leg by a lamppost, I'd like you to catch a clean sample of his urine in it. If you don't think you can manage that," he added, as my jaw hit the ground, "you can leave him with us for a couple of hours. We'll tie a plastic bag around his penis and collect the sample that way."

A minute later George went off happily with one of the nurses to be attached to a plastic bag. When I went back to collect him two hours later, he looked indignant, as well he might. The urine test result proved that there was nothing physically wrong with him. He wasn't ill and he didn't need therapy, the vet told me. It looked as if George was being naughty.

By the end of the following week I was in despair. My lovely home was being wrecked by the dog I adored. I knew I couldn't put up with the stench much longer. And yet the idea of getting rid of George was unthinkable. He was so much a part of our family now that to me he almost felt like another child. I say "almost," because deep down I knew that George wasn't a child. He was a dog, and a dog who had become impossible to live with. What could I do under the grim circumstances other than find him a new home where, one hoped, he'd be better behaved than he was in ours? But if I did that, I'd be heartbroken. To say nothing of Joshua. How could I take his dog away from him?

In tears, and unable either to sleep or work, I prowled around the malodorous flat one afternoon, wringing my hands and weeping as George trotted loyally behind me, merrily attempting to lick the body cream off my bare feet and unaware of my traitorous thoughts. There was nothing else for it, I decided, as I walked up the stinking stairs where we had discovered yet another puddle just the night before: George would have to go.

And that was when I caught the culprit in the act.

As George and I walked into the living room, she was squatting on the red velvet sofa in full stream, her cold eyes fixed on a faraway point. I gasped. Monster Mog! It had been her all along! Not only had she ruined the place, she'd let George take the rap. In fact, knowing her, she'd probably plotted the whole thing as part of a dastardly plan to get rid of him.

I ran toward her, full of murderous rage. "Don't you *dare!*" I shrieked. As I pushed her off the cushion, a stream of hot cat pee gushed off the velvet onto the rug and across my feet. Tail between his legs, George scurried out the room, worried that, as usual, he was about to be blamed for something he hadn't done. Furious at having been caught in the act, Monster Mog lashed out with her claws and flashed me a look of pure hatred. This is no more than you deserve, her expression said, for bringing that creature into my house!

I'd put up with so much from Monster Mog over the past eight years: her bad moods and unpredictability; her live frogs and dead or mutilated mice; her sustained violence toward George and her casual violence toward us. Now her reign of terror was at an end. Her attempt to get rid of the interloper had badly misfired. By pissing on her own doorstep, Monster Mog had shot herself in the paw.

It was time to find her a new, dog-free home, I decided, one where she'd be the center of attention. I offered her to Philip, who was convinced that her disgusting behavior was solely due to the fact that I didn't love her enough, or that I loved George too much, or both. Perhaps he and Sue would like to give her the affection and understanding she so obviously wasn't getting from me, I suggested. Surprisingly, they declined this once-in-a-lifetime opportunity. Perhaps it had something to do with their pristine white carpets and cream sofas.

What was I going to do with Monster Mog? I contemplated doing an Anthony — that is, putting her in a box, driving her to a distant destination, and releasing her — but I knew I couldn't. Besides, like Anthony's Norman, she might find her way back. No, I'd have to find my cat a loving new home. But who would want one with such terrible habits? I wouldn't have wished her on anyone.

In the end Greg advised me I had no choice but to take Monster Mog to an animal refuge. They there promised me faithfully that they would re-home her, and they did. The last I heard of her, her name had been changed to Tiddles and she was living contentedly with an elderly gentleman in a garden flat in the suburbs of South London.

Too far away from Hampstead to find her way back.

Fourteen

On June 3, 2001, Tabby, Hannah, Joshua, Nathaniel, and I marked the third anniversary of Udi's death in the same way that we'd marked the two previous ones: by taking George for a walk. Our destination was the wooden bench on Hampstead Heath that we'd dedicated to Udi's memory. In what was fast becoming an annual tradition, we took photographs of ourselves sitting there, let off some helium-filled balloons, and toasted Udi with champagne. We followed this with tree-climbing, including George, who scaled the lowest branches of the nearest oak tree, and finally a game of football, girls against boys. As usual, the two boys scored a hat trick, and knocked out us grown-up "girls" in the first five minutes, while a yapping George ran after the ball or cheerled on the sidelines for both teams.

It had been Udi's wish to be cremated rather than buried, so some time after his funeral we'd gone down to Kimmeridge, the beautiful Dorset bay on the South Coast where he'd spent so many happy days speedboating and windsurfing, and we'd scattered his ashes in the sea. In practice, this good-bye gesture turned out to be far less poignant than it sounds. A fierce gale was blowing, and instead of sinking gracefully into the sea the ashes flew back into our faces and over our clothes, which made us laugh as well as cry. It was just like Udi to be defiant to the last.

So there was no grave we could visit. There wasn't even a memorial plaque to Udi — for where that was meaningful to him could we have placed such a thing, other than in Camden Council's so-called "Parking Solutions" department? ("In memory of Udi Eichler," it could have read, "who died after a long battle against traffic wardens, owing the council £2000 in unpaid parking fines.") But before long my brother-in-law had come up with the imaginative suggestion that we dedicate a bench to Udi on Hampstead Heath. After a short search we'd found a perfect position facing the two small, spreading oaks where he'd often taken Joshua, Jessica, and Nathaniel climbing. Despite the winter view between the branches of the Royal Free Hospital — not only a hideous 1960s concrete eyesore but the place where Udi had been diagnosed and treated for cancer — it was a beautiful spot in a bright, open meadow where the long grass in summer was a mass of wild-flowers and butterflies.

I stopped at Udi's bench, as everyone in the family called it, whenever I took George to the Heath. In fact, he headed straight for it as soon as he was let off the leash, hurled himself onto the wooden seat, and waited for me to join him. "In loving memory of the one and only Udi Eichler" read the inscription. This might sound facetious to those who never knew Udi, but he would have appreciated it. After all, he'd certainly been a once-in-a-lifetime character. And he *had* had an unusual name. Unlike, say, a John Smith or a Jane Brown, I was pretty sure there'd only ever been one Udi Eichler — though neither of these names had originally been his. Even though he'd been born in Nazi-occupied Austria, he'd been christened a very British "Gerald" by his seventeen-year-old Anglophile mother, who'd actually wanted to name him Percy but was talked out of it by a friend. Rein-venting himself after he'd settled in England, the teenage Geri, as he was then known, had boasted to one of his friends that he was descended from an Austrian count named Udo Schaumburg von der Lippe. How close a relative he was to this count we will never know, but thereafter his friend called him Udi, a pet form of the Hebrew name Ehud, meaning "united," and the name stuck. As for Eichler, this had been the surname of his third stepfather, a man Udi remembered nothing about other than that he'd been a dancing instructor in Graz.

It was almost unbelievable that three years had passed since Udi's death. Sometimes it seemed so long ago that I felt it had happened in another life. At other times it seemed so close, and my recall of it was so raw, that it felt as if he'd died just an hour or two before. There were days when I could scarcely remember what his voice had sounded like, and though I'd been with him when he died, there were also days when I found it hard to accept that someone who'd once been so vital wasn't still alive. I'd see a man walking toward me down the road wearing a hat and glasses similar to the ones Udi had worn and stop in my tracks, certain for a split second that it was him. Or I'd hear a motorbike pulling up outside our house and run to the window, half-expecting to see Udi stride up the garden path in his "lederhosen" and crash helmet, with the silver and black Lurex scarf he'd been so attached to flung casually around his neck.

"I just can't believe I'll never see Dad again," Joshua said repeatedly, even though he already found it hard to remember much about the father he now hadn't seen for three years — a quarter of his own life. I knew exactly what he meant. I could survive without Udi, and even find a kind of happiness again, but that didn't stop me missing him more than ever. The first two years after I had lost him had had a certain momentum. Propelled into the role of a widow relatively young, I'd felt at times like the central character in a play — not one I'd ever wanted to star in, I hasten to add. Now the curtain had come down on it, and I was no longer a heroine who elicited people's sympathy: I'd reverted to being just another member of the audience. The drama of losing my husband was over. This was the rest of my life, and like Teresa Cornelys back in the eighteenth century, I had to stop moaning on the phone to my long-suffering sister, get my act together, and get on with it.

As for Joshua, three years down the line and about to turn twelve, he was becoming rather grouchy and introspective. Were his mood swings normal for a boy of his age, or was he secretly suffering in ways I couldn't begin to understand? Without Udi's special insight to guide me, I had to wait and see. Like other parents, I tried to ignore my son's occasional rudeness toward me, and attempted to stay cool when he flew off the handle or was less than charming to other adults. Sometimes I even succeeded. Deep down, I felt protective: after all, he had good reason to be angry with the world. As he himself once put it: "Other boys have real fathers. All I have is a bench on the Heath." Outwardly, though, I took a rather tough line and tried not to indulge him too much.

On the whole Joshua appeared to be coping brilliantly, and I was incredibly proud of him. But as he approached adolescence, I could tell that he needed a father's guidance more than ever. And more than anything, I still wanted to find a substitute father for him. So far I hadn't succeeded. I was probably expecting too much in hoping that I'd meet someone with whom I'd want to build a new life, and who liked me enough to want to take on me and my son. I'd been very lucky to meet Anthony, but that hadn't worked out. It seemed highly unlikely that I'd ever fall in love again.

It was three o'clock in the afternoon when I

stepped onto a Northern Line tube train at Leicester Square. I'd spent the day working in the London Library, in St. James's Square, and I was on my way to meet Joshua, who was due out of school at four. The carriage was practically empty, and I sat down and started to read through the notes I'd been making. For once, I was totally absorbed in my work.

Within a minute, the train had pulled into Goodge Street station. The doors opposite me slid open, and several people entered the carriage. Out of the corner of my eye I noticed a gray-haired man who must have been in his mid-fifties. He hesitated for a moment and then, although there were plenty of empty seats, he sat down next to me.

The doors closed and the train accelerated out of the station. Don't ask me why, but something made me look sideways at him across my notes. I caught sight of a pair of beige cotton trousers and two pale, finely boned hands emerging from the sleeves of a crumpled black linen jacket. On his lap he'd placed a large, well-worn, brown leather saddlebag. Through its open top I could see the untidy contents. There were several pens, a large bunch of keys, a packet of cigarettes, and — more interestingly — a typed manuscript corrected by hand in blue ballpoint pen.

It was this, I think, that aroused my curiosity. Maybe he was a writer, like me, I thought. As surreptitiously as I could, I glanced at what I could see of his face in profile. He had a long, aquiline nose, well-formed lips, and a rather furrowed, anxious-looking forehead that was half-covered with a mass of silver gray curls. His wasn't a particularly handsome face, but I found it interesting — no, more than that, compelling. It was a face that looked familiar to me, even though I'd never seen it before. A face that I instinctively wanted to know better. Suddenly he turned and our eyes met for an instant. I quickly looked away, feeling myself turn red. For it seemed to me that the stranger hadn't just looked into my eyes: he'd looked right inside me.

The train drew into Warren Street station. The doors opened and closed again. This time I wasn't aware of whether or not anyone else got into or out of the carriage. For a reason that I couldn't explain to myself, I was convinced that the man sitting next to me was the man at whose side I was destined to grow old. And, which was even more ludicrous, that he felt exactly the same way about me.

The London tube is a famously anonymous place. Passengers rarely talk to one another, perhaps because they're packed together like cattle most of the time. Plugged into their MP3 players or absorbed in a novel or newspaper, each does a brilliant job of pretending that no one else in the world exists. It's almost unheard of to strike up a conversation with your fellow travelers, and if it wasn't for the rattle of the carriages and the whine of the brakes, you could often hear a pin drop between stations. So when my neighbor suddenly tried to strike up a conversation with me, I knew he wasn't making small talk. It meant something.

"Excuse me," he said, "but do you know where this train's just come from?"

I was nonplussed. If this was an opening gambit, it was, I had to admit, a pretty poor one. Who in the world cares where a tube train's come from? The only important thing is where it's going to. "I've no idea," I said. My fellow traveler nodded, and cleared his throat nervously. I wanted to carry on the conversation, to say something equally fatuous, such as "Why do you want to know?" But I stopped myself. I wasn't in the habit of chatting up men on the tube. Women like me didn't do such things. This man was a stranger. For all I knew he was happily married. Or deeply disturbed. Or a violent rapist. Or a mass murderer. Or all four!

We traveled on in heavy silence through Euston, Mornington Crescent, and Camden Town stations. As we headed for Chalk Farm, I sensed him turn to look at me. A ridiculous scenario was playing in my head, like part of an old black-and-white movie. In it, I saw us sitting together at a table in an old-fashioned country-cottage kitchen. We weren't talking, just sitting at the table writing, in an atmosphere of comfortable companionship. Joshua was there. The man smiled at him. There was ease between them, just as there was between this man and me . . .

The scenario ended when the train pulled into Belsize Park and the man from my movie got up and walked to the doors. He turned and looked directly at me just before he got off the train. And, instead of walking away, he stood on the platform, staring at me quizzically through the open doors. He seemed to be willing me to get out of the train and join him.

I wanted to, more than anything. I knew that if I didn't I'd regret it deeply. This was my last opportunity to act — and it was fast running out. In a few seconds it would be gone forever.

I stayed where I was. The doors slid closed. The man gazed at me sadly. Then the train moved off, and he disappeared.

If destiny had decreed that I should meet my soul mate on a train, I'd dumbfounded it. I cursed myself for having been so conventional, so cowardly.

Next time I wouldn't let a chance like that slip away.

Fifteen

Later that summer I met Alex on a street corner — our street corner, as a matter of fact. I was loitering with George beside his favorite lamppost, enjoying the early evening sunshine, when he spotted a squirrel and yanked me off in pursuit of it.

"Sorry!" I said as I rounded the corner and crashed straight into a tall, solid, dark-haired man wearing a trench coat. He'd just got out of a convertible Mercedes, followed by a big black lurcher, and his arms were laden with carrier bags of food, one of which went flying across the pavement.

A pair of very round, very dark, and rather mischievous eyes glanced at me as I stooped to help him pick up his scattered shopping. "Look! You've broken my bottle of champagne!" he said, as a pool of white liquid leaked from the carrier bag,

"It looks like milk to me!"

As our two dogs lapped it up, we started

to chat. It turned out that we were neighbors. Alex, the divorced father of four children, had moved into a house just around the corner from mine about six months after Udi had died. Although I'd heard other people mention him, and he'd heard of me, we'd never actually met before — a typical London scenario. It also turned out that we came from remarkably similar backgrounds: both of us were middle-class Jewish North Londoners, who came from secular rather than religious families, and we'd been brought up several streets away from each other in the nearby suburb of Cricklewood.

We had something else in common, too: we were both in effect single parents. Alex's two sons and two daughters, who ranged in age from eight to fifteen, lived a couple of miles away with their mother for half of the time, but for the rest they lived with him and Rocket Ron, the lurcher he'd recently adopted from Battersea Dogs' Home.

I felt relaxed with Alex. He was a big-built, big-hearted man who emanated warmth and humor. Everything he said made me smile. Before we parted in the street, I heard myself say, "You must come round for supper sometime."

"Okay," he replied. "How about later this week?"

I named a day, but not without trepidation. I was more anxious about how Joshua would react to a male stranger being invited into the house than I was about how Alex would take to my domestic ménage, but I needn't have worried on either count. By the end of the evening, Joshua was perched on the sofa arm next to Alex, chatting to him about Arsenal Football Club, of which they were both passionate supporters. As for George, he was sitting on Alex's knees.

To say that Alex was child-friendly would be a gross understatement. Full of fun, generous, and indulgent, he seemed to be something of a child himself. He was also a fatherly man with whom children instantly felt safe and at ease. He and Joshua hit it off brilliantly.

We became friends. We talked on the telephone, chatting for hours about our lives and our children. Alex wanted to take things further, but I was apprehensive. What if we started seeing each other and it didn't work out? By then Joshua would have got more attached to him.

Then, one night, Alex and I went to see *Bridget Jones's Diary* at a local cinema. It felt so comfortable and right to be out together that I decided to throw caution to the wind, and we started dating.

Joshua warmed to Alex more and more. He liked his relaxed, "anything goes" manner and his penchant for the grand gesture, of which there were plenty. For he had recently sold out the computer business he'd been building up for years, and he had time on his hands and money to spend. There were family trips to Highbury in his convertible Mercedes to have lunch and watch Arsenal matches; and frequent meals in smart Italian restaurants; and an unforgettable day out at the Prince's Trust concert in Hyde Park, when we were collected from our home by a white stretch limo and found ourselves sitting in VIP seats in the row just below Prince Charles, who joked with us and shook Joshua's hand. This was very seductive to a young man who'd recently turned twelve and who'd lost his father.

As for George, he was in doggie heaven. Alongside Rocket Ron, who, despite standing almost six feet tall on his hind legs, was convinced he was a lapdog, George was allowed — no, encouraged — to trample over the furniture and curl up on people's knees at Alex's house. Then there were our walks on the Heath, where George trotted happily behind his new friend, a rescued racing dog who would suddenly take off at the scent of rabbit and gallop into the distance, leaping over fallen branches and tree stumps like a Grand National front runner at Aintree. Luckily for me, Ron was as disobedient and badly trained as George. Since it was impossible to catch him when he did a runner, Alex would go hoarse in his efforts to call him back. In the end he resorted to carrying a bag of chicken scraps in his pocket so that he could bribe Ron to obey him. And whenever Ron was given a treat, it seemed only fair that George should have one, too.

The way to a dog's heart is through his stomach, and here Alex scored a thousand extra points in George's eyes. It wasn't only the chicken treats. Take-out Chinese meals, eaten off a low coffee table in Alex's living room while the family watched football matches on satellite TV, meant there was always some tasty tidbit for a dog to snack on in his house. The garden provided even richer pickings: from May through October the barbecue seemed to be permanently going, and abandoned morsels of burger, chops, and sausage lay as thick on the lawn as the daisies.

Aside from the barbecues, than which there could be nothing better in a dog's eyes, George's other favorite activity with Alex was eating at restaurants. Alex loved going out for lunch on weekdays, and unless there was a full-scale downpour or the temperature was below zero, he liked to sit in the open air, which meant that the dogs could come with us. Roof down, Alex's Mercedes would set off from his house on the corner, then cruise to a halt outside mine — even though we lived four doors from each other, he believed in picking up his date. George clambered into the back alongside Ron, I got into the front, and with my Cavalier's ears flapping in the wind, we cruised off to any dog-friendly restaurant that had al fresco tables. Since Ron's pointed nose and beady eyes were on a level with our plates even when he was sitting down, he worked on making us feel guilty as we ate, while George barked and leaped up and down to make his presence felt, in case he was forgotten when the scraps were distributed.

As befitted a pampered pooch descended from royalty, George took to his new improved lifestyle as to the manner born. What self-respecting dog wouldn't have? As my father used to say, "It takes five minutes to get used to a better standard of living," and this standard suited our luxury-loving

Cavalier down to the chipolata-littered ground. But, like a young rock star who's suddenly come into the money, George's character changed, and not for the better. The good life had gone to his head. And everywhere else.

Since Monster Mog had been re-homed, George had blossomed into a much more self-assured dog. For a start, his fear of felines had gone. In fact, when it came to cats, George was now eager to prove that he was no longer a wuss. If he saw a cat in the street, he strained to get near it, barking madly until the poor thing turned tail and disappeared over the nearest wall, at which point George would swing round and grin at me excitedly. At home, he ran up and down stairs with wild abandon, as if determined to dispel the memory of Cerberus standing guard on the middle stair.

Since I'd felt so guilty about having blamed George for what had turned out to be Monster Mog's disgraceful puddles, I'd spoiled him thoroughly. But within months of my meeting Alex, George wasn't just spoiled, he was ruined. His eyes had a wild, almost feral glint, as if he couldn't believe his luck. Every time he was taken for a walk, he now dragged Joshua or me straight to Alex's front gate and refused to move any further. If we rang the bell and the gate clicked open, he charged into the garden and, pausing only to lift his leg briefly on a lavender plant and sniff around under the barbecue, galloped up to the front door and barked to be let in as if he owned the place. Once inside, he headed straight for Ron's bowl in the kitchen and licked it clean of whatever food it contained while Ron towered over him, mildly dismayed.

If I tried to lead George past Alex's house or, even worse, dared to walk him in the opposite direction, toward the Heath, he dug his claws into the paving stones and refused to budge, however hard I tugged at the leash. A walk was no longer acceptable, it seemed, if it didn't include Alex and his bag of treats. "Come ON, George!" I shouted, earning myself the disapproving looks of passersby. But George wouldn't move — unless, that was, he spotted a Mercedes, in which case he'd run up to it, then turn and stare at me with the arrogance of an A-list celebrity waiting for his chauffeur to open the door for him. As he cocked his head to one side, you could almost hear him say, *Are we lunching at the Italian in Belsize Park again? Can't we go to the Greek in Primrose Hill? I want lamb kebabs today!*

To help him communicate his wishes to

us, George developed a whole new vocabulary. He would snort insistently when he wanted something, yelp loudly for tidbits, whine with a high-pitched squeak to attract our attention when Alex and I were talking to each other, and grunt methodically and loudly while he was resting or even asleep, just to let us know he was there. All the extra food he was scoffing took its toll on his waistline, which, like the circumference of a slowly inflating balloon, grew bigger and rounder every day. As his belly swelled beneath his fur coat, he also became pinker. It took me weeks to work out why. Then, one day, I realized: my beautiful dog was turning into a pig.

Or was he? "Look, Mum! A sheep!" said a rude little girl in the street one morning, pointing at George. What was she talking about, I wondered, with the blindness of a mother who thinks her child is the most beautiful on earth. I was about to say, How dare you? when I caught sight of the animal waddling slowly behind me. Oh, my God, George *was* a sheep — a wild-looking, long-haired Highland sheep! At some point in the last year his coat had changed from the kind of sleek, glossy locks you see tossed about by models in shampoo advertisements into a long, thick, curly, dull, frizzy mane.

"What's happened to him?" I asked Greg, in front of whom I presented my canine-ovis crossbreed later that afternoon, hoisting him onto the examination table with arms that ached under his weight. "He looks like a pom-pom!"

"Ah well, yes, this does sometimes happen to male Cavaliers after castration," he said sagely, full of information long after the event. "The texture of their coat changes, and there's nothing you can do about it." He sank his fingers into the tangled jungle of George's hair and ran his hands down his body. "He's also put on a bit, hasn't he? I can't feel his ribs at all." Flicking a switch on the wall, he turned on the scales, which were situated underneath the examination bench. The digital display on the wall ran up faster than a London taxi meter, stopping only when it reached a whopping 10.45 kilos. "Hmm." He turned to his computer and checked back through George's records. "Let's see . . . Last time I weighed him he was under five kilos. And you were worried he was anorexic." He cleared his throat. "Well, your worries are over. George is now clinically obese."

"How is that possible?"

"How do you think? Dogs put on weight for the same reasons humans do. It's a question of too much food and not enough exercise. Has George been overeating lately? Snacking between meals, perhaps? Did you put him back on the all-in-one food after he'd recovered from eating that foam ball?"

"Er . . . sort of," I lied.

"Have you been adding extras to it?"

"Just occasionally," I admitted.

"Well, it'll have to stop. George needs to go on a diet. Starting now."

Poor George. I did feel sorry for him. He didn't take kindly to the supper of exorbitantly expensive low-calorie diet gravel that Greg prescribed for him. In fact, when I put it in front of him, he looked at me as if I'd gone mad. He plucked a single lump from the brown slag heap, moved it round in his mouth for a moment, spat it out onto the floor, and like the spoiled king he was, threw himself down in a sulk.

When Alex called to invite us round for a Chinese takeout that evening, I decided to leave George at home: the temptation of stir-fried crispy beef and sweet-and-sour prawns would be too much for him. Our departure provoked a volley of furious yapping. As we walked away from the house, he stood on the back of the sofa, nose pressed against the window, looking as if he'd been abandoned forever.

"I bet he's still sitting there," Joshua said as, stuffed to the gills, we walked guiltily home a couple of hours later. But as we came up the garden path, George's perch atop the sofa was conspicuously empty. And when we walked into the house, he was nowhere to be seen.

"George? George!" we called. Still, there was no welcoming patter of paws on floorboards, just a faint but furious barking from the garden.

"He's probably still sulking," I said. "Perhaps I've been too hard on him. Surely a few mouthfuls of Peking duck wouldn't have mattered?"

"Mum!"

We waited for George to come in, run upstairs, and greet us. He didn't. And when Joshua looked down on the garden from the kitchen window, he couldn't see him anywhere.

"I'm sure something's happened to him, Mum. I'm going down to find him."

"What could possibly be wrong?" I called after him as he left the room.

My answer was a frantic yell. "Mum! Come quickly!"

I flew downstairs. A shredded Kleenex box

lay in the middle of the hall, surrounded by a sea of massacred paper tissues. And the perpetrator was standing by the side door. Or rather, his hindquarters were standing by it. His front half was outside in the garden. George was stuck halfway through the cat flap.

"Oh, George! What's happened to you?"

As we knelt down beside his fat, fluffy bottom, George's tail started to wag frantically. Meanwhile, out in the garden, his head continued to bark.

Joshua and I fell to our knees. "He must have eaten too many tissues," I said. "He must have been hungry. I blame that diet food. His stomach's obviously swollen."

"Mum!" Joshua said. "Face facts — he's become huge!" He helped me try to ease George through the eight-inch-square opening, but with no success. Like a very round peg hammered into a square hole far too small for it, George was well and truly stuck. To make matters worse, his hair had caught in the hinges. "Get me some scissors, Mum," Joshua said, with all the authority of a senior accident rescue team member. "We'll have to cut him out."

After half an hour of snipping at him with my manicure scissors, we were finally able to push George through the cat flap. His hair looked as if it had been cut by a punk stylist wearing a blindfold: there were almost-bald patches, spikes, and uneven frizzy bits. Back in the house — this time through the spacious French windows — he rolled on the clumps of discarded hair that now littered the hall carpet, then stood up and galloped off, shaking vigorously. Not only did it take me ages to clear the hair up, it also clogged the vacuum cleaner, which had to be unblocked at vast expense.

Speaking of which . . . The following morning I took George to the nearest canine beauty salon for a cut and blow dry. At £40 his new hairdo cost almost as much as my own usually did. Shampooed, clipped, manicured, and groomed to within an inch of his life, he emerged looking less like the untidy Highland sheep he'd recently begun to resemble and more like the show dog I'd originally bought. Though distinctly on the chunky side, he was now as handsome as ever.

As if aware of the beauty that had been newly unveiled by his hairdo, George pranced friskily ahead of me on the Heath that afternoon, lapping up the admiring comments lavished on him by strangers, his tail held arrogantly high. I felt proud to be the owner of such a magnificent, glossy, clean animal. Until we reached the ponds.

It wasn't really George's fault. Even a human might have mistaken the thick carpet of algae and duckweed floating on the surface for a grassy field. Or perhaps George felt so cocksure of himself that he truly believed he could walk on water. For whatever reason, when he plunged into the pond he was a gleaming chestnut and white dog, and when he scrambled out he was emerald green. As were my white trousers by the time I'd hoisted him up the steep bank.

Shocked and invigorated by his unexpected cold dip, George ran around in wide circles, showering everyone within reach with slime. Then he threw himself down in a patch of dry mud and rolled on his back.

By the time he stood up, his coat was dark brown, his mouth was open in a very pink grin, and his eyes were glinting with the excitement of having discovered a brand-new game. The applause of the large audience who'd gathered around him egged him on to a further bout of mud-rolling.

George was nothing if not a crowd-pleaser. He'd play this game again.

Six months after we'd started seeing each other, the leisurely weekday lunches with Alex had ground to a halt because I was too absorbed in writing my book. This meant Alex and I could only meet up at weekends or in the evenings, which was easier said than done. For two people who lived less than fifty meters away from one another, finding time to be together was ridiculously hard. Between us we had five children, all of whom went to separate schools and were at different stages of their education. Since we were both very much "hands-on" parents, we felt duty-bound to be around to lend encouragement with exam and test revision, homework, and assorted school projects. Then there were school plays, concerts, and parent-teacher evenings. There were family birthdays galore, each with its own well-established rituals, which, in Alex's family, always included his ex-wife. There were times, too, when we simply wanted to *be* there for our children — to hang out with them, slob out with them in front of the television, and make sure they went to bed at a decent time.

When Alex and I did manage to spend a free evening together, we often had nowhere to be alone. In his house there were four children and their assorted friends. In mine, there were Joshua and his friends, Martina, and, more often than not, her friend Ivona. In order to be alone, Alex and I took to sitting on the public bench on the corner where our two streets met. "Look at us," he said one night, as we sat there with our respective dogs, drinking Coke out of cans and eating a packet of salt-and-vinegar crisps. "We own two houses in this street, but we're sitting here like a couple of vagrants!"

There was too much domesticity for both of us. It was hopeless trying to juggle it all in two separate homes, albeit virtually side by side. The only solution would have been for us to move in together, but that would have required a huge leap of faith on both sides, and an even bigger house than his, for there certainly wasn't room in my flat for Alex's four children, and unless two of his children were forced to share a bedroom instead of having one each — surely a recipe for disaster — there was no room for Joshua at his place either.

On paper, Alex and I seemed perfectly suited. But for some reason, unfathomable to either of us, our relationship wasn't happening. Fond as we were of each other, when push came to shove neither he nor I wanted to give up a home and the way of life we'd established in it. It was too much of a gamble, and I guess neither of us believed that the odds of success were high enough to warrant it. So we settled instead for a close friendship rather than romance — a valuable thing in its own right.

All good relationships come to an end. This time I suspected that Joshua would be very upset. He'd already told me that if he was ever to have a stepfather, he wanted it to be Alex, so I was apprehensive about breaking the news to him that we weren't going out anymore. Reassured, perhaps, by Alex's promise that he would continue to be there for him, Joshua reacted to the breakup in a far more dispassionate manner than I'd imagined he would. At twelve, he was emotionally stronger and, it seemed, more mature than I'd have thought possible in any boy of his age, let alone one who'd lost his father. I was unbelievably impressed by how he coped with the potentially difficult situation.

No, it was George who was devastated by the split. He couldn't understand why we'd stopped going to Alex's house, or why there were no take-out meals to pick at, or why chicken treats were no longer doled out liberally on the Heath. Every time we walked past Alex's front gate, he paused for a sniff, shot me an appealing look, and wagged his tail tentatively, as if to ask, Can't we go inside? When I walked on by, dragging him reluctantly behind me, his eyes took on a sad, wistful glaze, as if he was overcome with memories of barbecues past and rides in a silver Mercedes.

I, too, was sad that my relationship with Alex hadn't worked out, and not just because of those delicious barbecues. I knew I'd been incredibly lucky to meet someone as kind as he was — someone who had, above all, got on so well with Joshua — and I felt a terrible failure for not having pulled out the stops to make the relationship work. What was wrong with me? What more was I looking for, in my circumstances and at my age?

Sixteen

By the late spring of 2002 I'd come to the conclusion that it was time I put dating to one side again and learn to enjoy my own company. So far, I'd rather successfully avoided having to face the fact that I was by myself, but four years after losing Udi it was time surely that I grew up and got used to it. After all, I'd just turned forty-nine. It was almost unseemly at my age — not to mention unbelievably immature — to run around like some demented teenager in search of a second Mr. Right. There were far worse things in life than being single.

I hadn't stopped missing Udi during the last year — far from it — but instead of being a constant thorn in my side, grief had changed into a kind of dull, intermittent pain, like a throbbing toothache that flares up, hurts for a while, then fades away. Through force of circumstances I was now a different person from the one I'd been when he died. I was stronger, a little tougher perhaps, and certainly more self-confident. I'd gotten used to making my own decisions rather than waiting for him to take care of things in his own, larger-than-life, devil-may-care way. Since there was no one else to do it for me, I'd taught myself to change electric plugs, mend the broken hinges on cupboard doors, and check the car tire pressure. I'd even learned to deal with those monstrous spiders that materialize in the bath first thing in the morning: quickly, violently, and with my eyes half-closed.

I was okay because Joshua was okay. In fact, he was more than okay: he was flourishing. As he said on the fourth anniversary of Udi's death, "I still miss Dad, but I'm not unhappy with the way things are. I like our life together, Mum." I had a lot to be grateful for, this most of all.

At the beginning of August, I took my son to Paddington Station and waved him off to camp for a fortnight. As he disappeared onto the train in the company of his school friends and without a backward glance, I experienced a moment of panic. This was the first time I'd been without Joshua since Udi's death. What made me feel even more alone was that Sue was on holiday in France, most of my friends were away, and

Martina had temporarily returned to the Czech Republic to visit her family.

In anticipation, I'd dreaded being left in London by myself, but when it came to it I felt liberated. George was my constant companion, and I couldn't have had a better one, I decided, as he sat beside me on the garden bench, helping me to correct the all-but-finished manuscript of my biography of Teresa Cornelys by shredding the pages I deemed no good. Dogs were certainly easier to be with than boyfriends. They never remembered the nasty things you said to them or bore a grudge if you went out without them: the worst you might get was a few torn-up tissues on the floor when you returned home, which was, of course, the time when they were most delighted to see you. Dogs never complained. Unlike boyfriends, they loved and accepted you and your offspring unconditionally. Commitment phobia was unknown to them. No matter what you demanded of him, a dog would never walk out on you — unless, that was, someone turned up with a pocketful of treats, in which case you were, understandably, history.

A woman didn't have to worry about looking her best to impress a dog. Whether she was dressed to the nines or slopping around in a saggy old dressing gown first thing in the morning, it made no difference to how much her dog loved her — in fact, he probably preferred her the latter way, with an unwashed face and dog breath. Dogs didn't care whether your conversation was witty, repetitive, stupid, or plain boring; in fact, they didn't care if you said nothing at all. Dogs didn't groan if you cooked the same food day after day. They didn't nag to go out to the cinema at night, because they preferred to be slumped on the sofa next to you as you read a book or watched television — even then they had no preference for a documentary on environmental pollution over a repeat of *Sex and the City*. Only one thing mattered to them: that they were with you.

Freed of all domestic responsibilities for the first time in four years, I made two promises to myself. While Joshua was away, I wasn't going to do any cooking at all, except for the roast chicken I sprinkled sparsely over George's diet food: it was, I'd discovered, the only way to get him to eat it. And I would go out every night, even if it meant doing something alone. Before Joshua left London, I filled my diary: supper dates with old friends and acquaintances, trips to art galleries, theaters, and the cinema. There was just one evening in my diary — Wednesday the 7th of August — for which I had no plans, so I arranged to have a drink with a professor of art history. I wanted to check with him some of the facts in the manuscript of my book.

I'd never met Professor Zachary O'Neill, who lectured at the University of London. But six months previously, when I'd been searching the archives for a portrait of Teresa Cornelys, a friend of a friend had suggested I pick his brains about where to look. An American from Boston who spoke with a deep, sonorous drawl, Professor O'Neill had proved easy to talk to on the telephone, and he'd suggested a list of museums and private collectors who might be able to help me. As it turned out, they hadn't: no painted portrait of Teresa existed, or if it did, I was unable to trace it.

At the end of our conversation, Professor O'Neill had generously told me to feel free to contact him again if I needed to. Though I'd written one history book before — about Soho — and I'd studied British history when I'd trained as a London tourist guide in my post-student days, I didn't have a university degree in the subject; in fact, as an art school dropout, I didn't have a degree at all. This made me doubly anxious not to make any historical blunders when I wrote about the eighteenth century. The professor, I hoped, would be able to set me straight on a number of matters about art and architecture in Teresa's day.

By e-mail, I arranged to meet Professor O'Neill at seven p.m. in the bar at the St. George's Hotel in Regent Street. Later the hotel's name would seem rather ironic to me, but I chose the bar there because it was a little-known fifteenth-floor venue with fabulous views over London, where it was quiet enough to talk. I certainly couldn't have chosen a worse evening. One of the heaviest thunderstorms in recent history had settled over Southeast England that afternoon, with its epicenter over Northwest London, and an unprecedented sixty millimeters of rain — more than two inches — had fallen since four thirty. There were flash floods all over the city, and the Northern Line, my local tube route, closed down, as did many of the mainline stations. Hampstead was the site of a truly tropical monsoon, and for over an hour I feared I wouldn't be able to leave the house, even to get into a taxi — that is, if I could find one.

Eventually I did. As I sat in the otherwise deserted hotel bar, waiting for the professor to arrive, I didn't look or feel my best. My hair had been flattened on the short journey between my house and the cab, my mascara was masquerading as lip liner, and I could think about nothing other than my precious son. The bar's plate-glass windows looked westward across the rain-drenched rooftops of Marylebone toward the area outside London where Joshua was camping. The clouds over that way were a filthy gray, and lightning continued to flash in the distance. If the weather at the campsite was half as bad as it was in London, it would be a washout.

Suddenly the door opened, and a man in his mid-fifties walked in. I did a double take: he was Mr. Belsize Park, the man I'd met on the Northern Line. No, he wasn't: he just looked like him. Of medium height and slight build, he was wearing a rather stylish, pristine beige trench coat and carrying a very wet black umbrella. Just a little taller than I was, he had piercing dark eyes and an interesting face with slightly irregular features, topped by silvery gray curls. Since he was alone, and looking around curiously, I assumed he must be Professor O'Neill, so I stood up and introduced myself.

He raised his eyebrows. "You're Judith?"

"You seem surprised."

"To be honest, I am. It's crazy, but from

the formal tone of your e-mail I'd imagined you to be more of a Miss Marple figure — thirty years older than you are, in thick tweeds, elastic stockings, and brogues!"

"Oh, I only wear those on special occasions."

He laughed, took off his coat, folded it carefully, hung it over the back of a chair, and sat down opposite me. After I'd ordered some drinks — vodka on the rocks for him and, as I had questions to ask him and had to stay sober, sparkling water for me — I sat down beside him and we started to talk.

Two hours later we were still talking, I was on to my second glass of Chardonnay, and we hadn't yet broached the subject of the eighteenth century. Did I care? Fifty-five-year-old Professor O'Neill — Zach — was nice. He was really nice, actually: friendly, amusing, and interesting. And attractive. Though he was obviously very clever, he didn't feel the need to thrust his knowledge at me. An American of Irish descent, he'd been born and brought up in Boston, Massachusetts, and had moved to England thirty years before, when he'd met the Englishwoman who'd later become his wife. They'd been divorced for fifteen years, and since he'd recently broken up with a long-term girlfriend, it turned out that

Zach, like me, was on his own.

What was most alluring about him was that he wanted to know all about me. As the wine took effect — I'd never learned to hold my alcohol — I realized I was flirting with him in a rather obvious manner. Why was I doing this? I asked myself. I'd given up trying to find Mr. Right, and I'd just got used to being Ms. Happily Single.

I jumped up and grabbed my coat. "Oh, my God, look at the time! Zach, I've kept you long enough! Listen, I really must be going." I snatched up the bill that the waiter had left on the table. "I'll take this."

He reached for it. "Please . . ."

"No, I insist. Thanks so much for coming, and all the advice about the book and every-thing."

He looked rather bewildered. "But I haven't given you any!"

"Oh?"

"You haven't asked me anything yet."

"Oh. I suppose not. I knew that second glass of wine would be fatal." We both smiled. "Perhaps I could e-mail my ques-tions to you?"

"Okay . . ." His dark eyes met mine. "Look, do you have to go now? I mean, do you have other plans? I'm famished. Perhaps I could buy you dinner? You can quiz me on the eighteenth century while we eat."

I never did. Over plates of upmarket bangers and mash in a nearby American-style diner ("I sure am pleased — I thought at first you might be a vegetarian," he said, as I tucked into some sausages.) the list of questions was forgotten, and I entertained Zach with stories about my family. He seemed genuinely interested in everything I said. And we shared exactly the same sense of humor.

"Thanks so much," I said when, two hours later, we parted on a corner halfway down Regent Street. "It was really nice to meet you."

"And you. I haven't had such a great time in ages."

"Me neither. Well . . . good-bye, then."

I offered him my hand, which he clasped in his own. Though it was a delicately boned hand, his grip felt warm and firm. His eyes looked directly into mine. "Would you like to have dinner with me again?" he asked.

He rang me three days later, and we chatted for ages. "So, are we going to see each other?" he asked.

"Okay," I agreed, somewhat cautiously.

"When?"

The following Saturday, he took me to a

restaurant in the ancient, but now trendy, Clerkenwell district of London, just behind Smithfield, the main wholsesale meat market in London. After we'd eaten, I took him on a walking tour of the surrounding maze of streets. Like the many American tourists I'd once guided round London, Zach had a passion for London's history, but he knew precious little about this particular area. I showed him my favorite church: St. Bartholomew the Great, built by the Normans in the twelfth century and tucked away behind the meat market. I also explained how Wat Tyler, the leader of the Kentish Rebels, rode out to meet the young King Richard II at Smithfield during the Peasants' Revolt of 1381. Wat's insolent attitude had earned him a sword slash on the neck from the Lord Mayor of London, and as he lay dying, the fourteen-year-old king rode his horse across to the rebels, told them he had just knighted Wat, and promised to give in to their demands, which included abolishing serfdom and ending the poll tax. As soon as they'd dispersed, Richard went back on his word. "Serfs ye are and serfs ye shall always remain," he is supposed to have said.

While I acted this out in my most dramatic fashion, Zach gazed at me with an indulgent smile. "I don't know why you came to me

for advice on history," he drawled. "*You* appear to know all about it."

Then he took me in his arms.

SEVENTEEN

A month later, Zach and I sat opposite one another in an Italian restaurant in South Kensington. We'd been to a lecture at the Victoria and Albert Museum, given by one of his colleagues, and were grabbing a meal on our way home. In the past few weeks my professor of art history had been pursuing me. Playing it cool hadn't come into it. This was the fifth time we'd seen each other, and I hadn't yet asked him a single question about the eighteenth century. Between our meetings we'd had countless hour-long telephone conversations, always instigated by him. I couldn't help being flattered and excited by all the attention he was paying me. It was incredibly romantic to be wined and dined by a suave American as if I was some kind of siren rather than a forty-nine-year-old mother. Zach made me feel young and desirable.

Since he'd only recently broken up with

his ex-partner, Zach was staying with friends while he searched for a new flat to buy. And since I didn't want to introduce him to Joshua until I had a better idea of what was happening between us, I deliberately hadn't invited him back to Hampstead. Consequently, our entire relationship, such as it was, had been conducted in cafés, bars, and restaurants — neutral territory, far removed from the complications of our lives. We were floating in a beautiful bubble — one that came complete with waiters and bottles of wine — and we were so perfectly happy in it that neither of us could imagine it would ever burst.

"What do you really want out of a relationship?" he asked me now, as we gazed at each other across the pizza.

I thought about it for a moment. "Love and companionship, I suppose. Someone to share my life with. And you?"

"Love and companionship. Someone to share my life with. And I guess some passion wouldn't go amiss!"

We clasped hands across the table. Our fingers intertwined. At that moment, we knew instinctively that we were in it for the long term. We were so happy when we were together. We never ran out of things to talk about. We laughed all the time. We felt like two halves of a whole. I could scarcely believe what was happening.

So carried away were we by that perfect moment that neither of us thought to define what we actually *meant* by "companionship" or what "share my life" really encompassed. Later this would become all too clear.

And there was something else we were conveniently not discussing: Zach hadn't yet met Joshua. And he hadn't had to deal with George.

At thirteen, Joshua as the angry Hamlet of yore was long gone. He now had his own interests to pursue, above all skateboarding, an activity that drew him to the center of London on most weekends and during the school holidays. Down on the South Bank of the Thames, he and his friends practiced their tricks on the pedestrian forecourt of an office building near Waterloo station, where they were regularly relieved of their sandwich money and mobile phones by the local muggers. Back across the river, they invaded deserted underground car parks in the City of London and annoyed the attendants there by racing up and down the concrete ramps.

At other times, the skateboarders took over our narrow, quiet Hampstead street.

They scooted down the road at top speed, leaped into the air just outside our house, kick-flipped their boards over, and crashed them down on the edge of a three-meter-long metal box that they'd rescued from a dump and now kept in our front garden: an object of beauty to rival the resurgent weeds. In my bid to be the perfect mother I tolerated this eyesore, and the banging made by all that "nollying" and "grinding," as their skateboarding tricks were called. But many was the time when I cracked and ran outside, screaming that they had to stop before they drove me, not to mention our amazingly tolerant neighbors, stark raving bonkers.

When Joshua eventually met Zach one Saturday afternoon, he greeted him in a polite manner that would have astounded Anthony, then disappeared to skateboard. It seemed that he no longer felt threatened by his mother having a boyfriend, if you could apply that term to a fifty-five-year-old, gray-haired professor. Instead, Joshua took it on trust that my male companions were tangential to my existence, while he remained at its core. At best, boyfriends meant trips to football matches and extra Christmas presents; at worst, it was probably faintly embarrassing to have a mother who went on dates.

But Joshua now knew for certain who the most important man in my life was: himself. Even George came second.

During the first year of our relationship, Joshua didn't see much of Zach: my new partner wanted me all to himself. As I wanted to spend time alone with him, too, and Martina was still living with us, I took advantage of having a live-in babysitter to allow my new relationship to develop outside my domestic sphere. Since he was in the middle of writing a book on French artists of the early nineteenth century, Zach was often out of the country, doing research or attending one of the many academic conferences he was invited to. Sometimes Tabby or my mother would come to stay with Joshua for a few days, and I'd join Zach in Paris or Rome for a weekend. If I couldn't get away, or he was going on a long-haul trip, he always brought me back a beautiful gift: a rope of pearls from a conference in Singapore, a scarf made of old kimonos from Chicago, earrings from Paris.

But in the summer of 2003, this idyllic situation changed when Martina packed up her vast collection of black leather shoes and boots and, with Ivona, from whom she proved inseparable to the last, returned to the Czech Republic to try to establish the legal career for which she'd originally trained. After living with us for two and a half years, she felt almost like a daughter to me, and I was heartbroken to see her go. I took on another au pair for a few months, but it didn't work out: neither Joshua nor I had anything to say to her, and I missed Martina and her friend Ivona and the vicarious pleasure I'd derived from having two young Czech glamour-pusses lounging around the house discussing their social lives. When I talked the situation over with Joshua, we came to the conclusion that we no longer wanted to share our house with a stranger: we wanted it for ourselves. He was of an age when he neither needed nor wanted a babysitter if I went out for a few hours in the evening, and when I thought about it, I realized that the main reason I still had an au pair was to help me take care of George. That was ludicrous.

Once Joshua and I were on our own, however, I discovered that going out at night was more problematic than I'd thought it would be. Although he was happy to be by himself, I didn't like leaving him, particularly on weeknights, and I certainly didn't like staying out late. If he was at a friend's house or had people over, that was one thing. But if he was alone at home, perhaps struggling with his homework, I felt guilty for not being with him. Instead I wanted Zach to spend more time up in Hampstead with us.

As I gradually came to understand, this wasn't what Zach had had in mind when we'd talked so romantically about sharing our lives in that pizza restaurant. He'd wanted someone who could stay late at midweek dinner parties, someone who was free to travel with him, someone who'd spend time alone with him at his new flat in Hackney, the cosmopolitan, up-and-coming area of East London to which he'd recently moved. What I'd meant by sharing our lives was building a life together which naturally included Joshua and George and, to a lesser extent, my extended family. For the first time since we'd met, there was tension between us. And it was set to get worse.

Zach liked Joshua very much — in fact he respected his quick mind, his sense of humor, and his easygoing character. However, he was at heart an intellectual with zilch interest in skateboarding and football and an aversion to *Big Brother* and *The Simpsons,* so there was little common ground between them. Although Zach adored his daughter, who was now in her late twenties, he had no experience of relating to teenage boys — not always the most communicative creatures at the best of times. To make matters worse, the people he mixed with socially either didn't have children or, like him, had children who'd flown the nest long ago. Like them, Zach had few domestic ties and didn't want any more.

He certainly didn't want to be tied down to a dog.

EIGHTEEN

I was about to learn a harsh fact of life: juggling children and boyfriends was hard when the man in your life and your child were not related, but juggling a child, a boyfriend, and a dog was impossible.

Some men, I'd heard tell, liked their partner's dog. Some men liked their partner's dog enough to allow it to sleep in the bedroom, even on the bed. One man I knew let his wife's dog sleep between them under the covers. (I won't name names here; he knows who he is.) Another cut off the legs of his marital bed to make it easier for his wife's geriatric mutt to leap onto it. And when even the legless bed proved too high for the old boy, he built a miniature staircase — carpeted, naturally — so that Fido could stagger up to the mattress and no longer had to jump.

There were men in the world who acquired dogs of their own volition. Alex was one. Another was Ken, who worked for our local council, and was out in all weathers, sweeping up fallen leaves, picking up litter, and generally keeping the streets of Hampstead village sparkling clean. A few years before, Ken had adopted a beautiful, friendly Alsatian–golden retriever cross called Tommy, after the dog's former owner died. Unless it was extremely cold out, Tommy accompanied Ken on his daily rounds of Hampstead, often dressed in a warm plaid dog coat. He was adored by the local residents and shopkeepers, who slipped him treats, stroked him, and kept an eye on him if he wandered off. Thanks to Ken, he'd become the most famous dog in the village.

While walking George on the Heath, I'd met a retired businessman with two Jack Russells, a male artist with a bouncing Labradoodle, and a man with a basset hound named Bozo who so enjoyed talking to me about his canine other half that he'd even asked me out for dinner. I thought I was on to a winner there, but alas, it turned out that the man didn't want to talk about anything *but* Bozo, and the subject of bottom sniffing as a method of greeting, when discussed over a plate of watery lasagne, wasn't conducive to human romance.

I once had a conversation with a very cool, attractive musician on Parliament Hill. Though he didn't have a dog with him, he confessed how much he still missed Rover, his retriever, which had died ten years before. Every now and then, he said, he put his entire family into the car, headed north to the pet cemetery near Manchester where Rover was buried, and picnicked on his grave. A little over the top? Perhaps. But at least the man wasn't cynophobic, as my new boyfriend appeared to be.

"I do *not* have a phobia about dogs," Zach insisted one night when I accused him of it.

"You do! I just saw you recoil when George came up to greet you. He was wagging his tail, Zach — he wasn't going to bite you!"

"Look, darling, I'm not *scared* of dogs. I just don't like them near me."

His attitude was in stark contrast to that of his parents, Doris and Joe, who owned a beautiful, waggy-tailed black Labrador-cross. When he was a puppy, they'd found him sitting in their garden one morning with a note attached to his collar: "Please look after him," it read. "I can't take care of him anymore." Moro, as he was called, was so grateful to have been adopted by Doris and Joe that he'd guarded their house ever since. He followed them faithfully from room to room, sat at their feet while they watched television, and slept beside their bed at night. In turn, Doris and Joe were so devoted to Moro that they never left home without him. They even refused to go to a restaurant unless he was allowed in, too. Unfortunately their dog-loving genes must have skipped a generation, for although Zach's daughter took to George when she met him, their son didn't.

Sensing that his owner's new human best friend would like to see her canine best friend out of the picture, or at least marginalized, George decided to win Zach over. He jumped onto his lap whenever Zach and I were sitting together on the sofa, causing Zach to leap up, flapping his hands and shouting, "Get it off me!" as if he was being attacked by a giant, man-eating leech. He trailed Zach slavishly around the flat, accidentally tripping him a couple of times in the process; Zach said George was even more of a menace than the sneakers Joshua left lying about. Attracted as much to the clothes as the man, George snuggled up in Zach's clean jacket if he accidentally left it lying on a chair, and laid his adoring head on Zach's crisply ironed trousers when he folded them up on the window seat at night.

Even after I'd spent hours brushing these garments clean, Zach would still be holding them at arm's length, squinting at them in search of stray hairs and nonexistent fleas.

Even George's most affectionate and ingratiating gesture — compulsive licking — didn't go down well with Zach. In vain did I explain that George was paying him homage, and invoke biblical, artistic, and historical precedents including Tintoretto's painting of *Christ Washing the Feet of His Disciples,* and Queen Elizabeth I washing those of her lowly subjects on Maundy Thursday. Zach merely shuddered, called for disinfectant, and when he thought I wasn't looking, drew a rather Leonardo da Vinci–esque doodle of an imaginary machine that turned live dogs into sausage strings.

Some might think it reasonable for a man to demand a few hours of privacy with his girlfriend. Zach was one of them. George was not. On nights when Zach slept over, my pooch found himself inexplicably banned from my bedroom on the grounds that his mere presence there made it impossible for Zach to go to sleep. While Martina was still living with us, George sometimes ended up on her bed, but once she'd left, he was forced on these nights to sleep by himself. Lonely and fed up, he prowled the flat at night, his claws clattering on the wooden floors upstairs. Descending to the downstairs hall, he snuffled at the crack under my closed door, then scratched and scrabbled noisily at the paintwork. Before long, he taught himself to operate the door handle, God knows how, and thereafter broke in at will, usually when Zach was walking around in his underwear. From then on George was no longer allowed the run of the flat at night. Instead he was banished to my study.

This was the room where he had once shared Martina's bed, and where he now happily sat, or rather dozed, all day long when I was working on my next book — a biography of the great eighteenth-century lover and adventurer Giacomo Casanova and the women in his life. Not only did George have the use of its comfortable human-size daybed, which was adorned with a blue fleecy blanket and feather-filled cushions, he also had his snug basket in there, too. But from the fuss he kicked up at being shut in the study at night, you'd have thought I'd locked him in a prison cell. George simply wouldn't accept his incarceration. He protested at regular two-minute intervals, just as he'd done in the bathroom on the first night he'd come to live with us. Letting him out then had been a huge mistake, I now saw. As my mother had warned me at the time, I'd made a rod for my own back and had no one but myself to blame.

This went on for month after month. Time after time I tried to teach my old dog the new trick of sleeping without me, but my haphazard methods of instruction — persuasion, bribery, and the occasional yell — seemed to have no effect whatsoever. George barked and barked until Zach, Joshua, and I could stand it no longer. Joshua tried taking him into his bedroom, but that wasn't good enough for George. He wanted me.

"Can't I let him in here? Please!" I begged Zach at two o'clock one morning when all three of us were still wide awake.

"No way. He snores. And he grunts. You know I can't sleep if he's in here."

"You can't sleep *now,* darling," I said, trying the pragmatic approach. "No one can. If he carries on like this all night, Joshua will be too tired for school and I'll be too tired to work."

"What about me? I've got to give two lectures tomorrow! Or rather, today. You have to train him, Judith."

"I'm doing my best."

"So you've been saying for the past — what? — a whole year!"

"Can't I start again tomorrow? He's been barking since midnight."

"Well, go and tell him to stop!"

I hauled myself out of bed, plodded down the hall, and opened the study door. George was standing right behind it. He hurled himself at me like a child who'd been separated from his mother during a ten-year war. "Be quiet, George!" I hissed, as he ran in overexcited circles around my ankles, making little crying sounds and trying to leap into my arms — a hopeless task, considering his girth. "Just go to sleep, will you? Sorry, but you can't come out of here!" As I turned to go, his muzzle dropped open as if he couldn't believe I was abandoning him so soon after our happy reunion.

Back in bed, I lay awake waiting for George to start barking again. Several minutes later, he did. I went out, told him off, and returned to bed. When he next barked, it was Zach who leaped to his feet. I could almost see the steam coming out of his ears. "Right! I've had it!" he hissed, making for the door.

"Where are you going?"

"To deal with him!"

The study door clicked open and I heard him shout menacingly, "Shut up, George! Or you'll end up at the dog pound!" I caught my breath. George must have, too, because he was suddenly silent. I heard the study door click. "See? You've just got to be firm with him," Zach said as he got back into bed beside me.

"Thanks," I murmured lamely.

"Don't mention it." He buried his head under the covers. "Next time I stay here I'm bringing earplugs!"

I think he fell asleep then. I didn't. Neither did George. Ten minutes later he started up yet again — only this time his protest was less of a bark and more of a pitiful yelp. Terrified he might wake Zach and Joshua, I sprang out of bed, tiptoed from the room, and dashed to the study. This time when I opened the door George was sitting on the daybed whimpering. He rolled his big dark soulful eyes in my direction. He looked so frightened and upset that I found it impossible to be cross with him. Instead, I sat down beside him, stroked his little round head, and tried to reason with him. After all, Cavaliers were supposed to be intelligent dogs.

"Look, George, darling, just *go to sleep.* Okay? You're quite safe here. I'm only two doors away. I haven't abandoned you. You like this room! I tell you what, I'll put on the radio, and you won't feel so alone. Now, isn't that nice? It's the World Service — very interesting. So just be quiet, will you? Please! If you know what's good for you! Don't you want nice Uncle Zach to like you? There's a good boy!"

I lay down next to him for a minute, and he began to settle. As did I. His nodding head fell slowly onto the cushions. As did mine. His eyes closed. As did mine. When I next opened them, the dawn light was peeping through the curtains and an angry Zach was standing over me in his dressing gown.

"Hmm," he said. "I see you'd rather spend the night with your dog than with me."

Similar scenes took place all too often. Zach refused to go to sleep if George was in the bedroom, and George wouldn't sleep if he wasn't. By the end of 2004, the special relationship between Man and Dog, famed from prehistoric times, had grown distinctly tricky down our way. To say nothing of the relationship between Man and Woman.

Long gone were the heady days when Zach and I had believed that nothing would ever come between us. It already had, in the shape of a cute Cavalier King Charles Spaniel.

NINETEEN

At four hundred and forty feet above sea level, Hampstead is the highest point in London. The leafy, picturesque village — for, though it was absorbed into the city's suburbs long ago, so it is still known — has been popular since the eighteenth century, when the middle classes flocked there from the polluted metropolis to drink the health-giving chalybeate springwater at the local spa. Though the waters did little good to the Romantic poet John Keats, who, by the time he moved to Hampstead in late 1818, was probably already suffering from the tuberculosis that had killed his brother, the rural atmosphere of the village inspired him to write some of his greatest poetry, including "Ode to a Nightingale."

Over the years, countless writers, musicians, and artists have been attracted to and inspired by the village and its vast Heath, the 791 acres of hilly meadows, woods, ponds, and copses that have long been known as "the Lungs of London." They included artists John Constable, George Romney, Henry Moore, Ben Nicholson, and Barbara Hepworth; the late great cellist Jacqueline du Pré, her pianist husband Daniel Barenboim, and maestro Alfred Brendel; and writers John Galsworthy, Daphne Du Maurier, and more recently, Margaret Drabble and John le Carré.

Being a "Hampstead novelist" or a "Hampstead intellectual" has long been a well-known cliché in British society, so when Udi and I moved to Hampstead in 1990, when Joshua was one year old, we both fell neatly into the trap. Udi had wanted to live in the area ever since his early twenties, when he'd fallen in love with a house in one of the village's most famous streets, Downshire Hill. At the time he'd been unable to raise the £8000 needed for the price tag in what was then an enclave of socialists and left-wing thinkers, but by the time we'd moved here, the same house was on the market for approaching half a million pounds, and most of the local socialists had long ago sold out to bankers and businessmen. Unable to afford such an outlandish price, we'd eventually settled for a smallish run-down duplex flat in a dilapidated Victorian house.

Lived in by an actress (she was a former James Bond girl), the flat was in appalling condition, as my father was quick to point out when he first came to view it. "There's nothing here!" he said in a scandalized voice. "Not a cupboard! Not a useable lavatory! Not a decent floor! Not a kitchen! Not a straight wall! You must be mad! What have you bought?" With our tails between our legs, Udi and I set about restoring it. Five months later, when my father next returned to see it, the flat had been transformed.

We both adored living in it, and equally we loved being in Hampstead. In fact, we felt as if we were on a permanent holiday. In his inimitable way, Udi soon got to know everyone in the neighborhood, along with their intimate personal histories. The open spaces of the Heath were on our doorstep, and our road was incredibly quiet. Yet the bustling High Street, with its plethora of shops and cafés, was only five minutes walk away — or one minute on Udi's motorbike, which, to my dismay, my eccentric husband often rode into the village early in the mornings, to pick up fresh bread and collect our newspapers, clad only in his voluminous dressing gown.

As well as taking our Boxing Day walks

with Tabby and Hannah, Udi and I often strolled across Hampstead Heath during the long summer evenings, with Joshua following behind us on his tricycle (once, we were so busy admiring the view that he fell into a pond and we didn't even notice). But it wasn't until after Udi's death, when I acquired George, that I really grew to love the Heath as much as I do now. For 353 days every year, the place is a haven of tranquillity. If it wasn't for the distant thrum of traffic, all who walked across it could easily believe themselves to be in deepest rural England. In the early mornings the muddy paths that crisscross the fields and cut through the woods, are the haunt of well-toned Lycra-clad joggers, who flash past clutching a bottle of Evian in one hand and an iPod in the other. They're followed at a slightly slower pace by hardy middle-aged men and women with damp towels rolled up under their arms, walking back from one of the open-air single-sex swimming ponds to which these diehards make pilgrimage every day of the year. If the water freezes over in winter, they simply break the ice and plunge in as usual. The afterglow of a swim in sub-zero temperatures, they tell me, is as good as seven gin and tonics, only without the hangover.

Then come the parents, shepherding their children from Highgate and Dartmouth Park to Hampstead's schools; groups of intrepid foreign tourists hiking through the woods to historic Kenwood House, their crisply folded maps clutched in their hands; nurses from the Royal Free Hospital in South End Green, enjoying a sandwich and a breath of fresh air in their lunch hour; the Heath keepers, cruising past in their bottle green pickup trucks; and even, sometimes, the occasional military horse rider, who has trotted up from the King's Troop barracks in St. John's Wood, smartly kitted out in jodhpurs and hard hat. And finally, dog walkers like me, or professionals with eight or nine leads hanging around their necks and their great packs of assorted mutts.

Although few people brave the Heath on cold winter nights, the long, hot summer evenings often bring out quite a crowd. Groups of young men play football. Lovers sit entwined on the benches or tangle passionately in the shadows under the trees. Friends meet in the meadows to play cards and eat sushi out of see-through plastic containers, their bottles of beer or wine spread around them on the grass. Often someone produces a guitar and starts playing — old Bob Dylan numbers seem a favorite.

Three times a year, however — on the Easter, Whit, and August bank holiday weekends — the peaceful nature of Hampstead Heath changes. You wake up one morning to find that a couple of caravans have pulled into the car park just above the ponds. Next, more caravans arrive at the top of the hill, and lines of heavy trucks roll down the incline, each bearing a generator and sections of machinery. There are huge iron girders painted scarlet, cobalt blue, and chrome yellow, and glass-sided booths etched with Victorian designs, and oily bits of crank shaft, and amplifiers, and giant teacups, and sections of hoardings upon which are painted the words "Dodgems" and "Ghost Train."

By the following day the west side of the Heath has been transformed. Instead of just trees, there are Twisters and Chair-o-Planes. There's a helter-skelter, a Waltzer, and a big wheel balanced precariously on small blocks of wood. There's a children's merry-go-round in the shape of a caterpillar, another with tiny airplanes, a bouncy castle, and a giant, Barbie-pink inflatable slide. Strings of colored lightbulbs hang between the trees like necklaces, and there are shooting booths, coconut shies, and food stalls where before there were only gravel and grass.

Hampstead's thrice-yearly fun fair has arrived. And for the next four days life in the old place won't be the same.

The sound of the thrill-seekers' screams, accompanied by the loud throb of music from huge boom boxes, is enough to send most Hampstead residents running for cover on bank holidays — unless, of course, their children drag them to the fair, as Joshua used to do to Udi and me when he was little. But even if you stay at home, it's impossible to escape from the racket. As you sit in your living room — windows closed, Beethoven turned up on the CD player, television tuned to *Pop Idol* — you can still hear the yells, the rap music, and rising above them, a sadistic male voice amplified by a Tannoy system: "The faster it gets, the more you screams! And the more you screams, the faster we goes!"

Though I still hankered now and then for a sticky mouthful of the candy floss I'd enjoyed when my father took me to the fair during my own childhood, I now tended, like most locals, to avoid the Heath on bank holidays. Since I was in the highly privileged position of having the place almost to myself for most of the year, I didn't enjoy walking there when the fair was on — unlike George, who shuffled along with his nose to the ground in search of discarded food. So on Easter Monday, March 28, 2005 — the date is indelibly branded in my mind — I decided to skip George's morning walk.

Actually, the fair wasn't my only reason for skipping it. I was cross with George, and I was very distressed about Zach. Things weren't good between us — and George wasn't the only problem. It was now more than two and a half years since we'd first met, but instead of our relationship moving forward, we found ourselves entrenched in a rut. I still longed for Zach to spend more time with Joshua and share the ups and downs of family life with me. He, on the other hand, wanted to shrug off the domestic coil completely and get back to the idyll of our first weeks together — a romantic enough aim, but an impractical one. It involved me spending a lot of time at his flat and going on holiday alone with him, and for a single mother with a dog this wasn't realistic.

Since Martina had returned to the Czech Republic, I'd been juggling what was in effect two separate lives — one as Joshua's mother, the other as Zach's partner — and it had felt more and more uncomfortable. It was as if I were trying to squeeze myself into a pair of beautiful jeans that were the wrong size and the wrong shape. If I held my breath, I could just about yank up the zip, but the unavoidable truth was that they didn't fit. Recently they'd been feeling tighter and tighter.

I was still hard at work researching and writing my new book about Casanova. Meanwhile Joshua, who was now fifteen, was studying for important school examinations. He was weighed down with homework, and his pre-exam nerves were frazzled. Our fridge had to be stocked with food, meals had to be on the table, and of course, George needed to be bathed, played with, and walked several times a day. I also wanted to make time to see my mother, my sister, my stepdaughters, and all my friends. There simply weren't enough hours in the day, or days in the week, to do everything and see everyone — and to please Zach as well.

Lately, as I'd driven manically from Hampstead to Hackney and back again of an evening, trying to placate him, I'd been feeling torn and utterly miserable. This wasn't how I wanted to live, cut up into little pieces. First and foremost I was a mother. Until my teenage son grew up and flew the nest, I wanted to be there for him, in our home, and I yearned for a partner who'd relish being there with me, rather than putting up with it under sufferance. But as far as Zach was concerned, this was a no-no. The very idea of making our relationship more domestic turned him off. I kept hoping that he'd change, and take a more active interest in my family, in particular in Joshua. They both seemed to like each other, but as far as I could see, they wanted little to do with one another. Instead of drawing closer to my son with time, Zach was moving further away from him. Sometimes when he came over, he and Joshua scarcely spoke. It was getting to the point where I simply couldn't bear the atmosphere in the house.

Perhaps our relationship was approaching its sell-by date. I hoped not. Despite the growing tension between us, I still loved my quirky American professor. At his best he was witty, urbane, romantic, and such stimulating company that I was never bored when I was with him. Though we came from completely different backgrounds, I felt remarkably at ease with him — when we weren't quarreling. In many ways we'd become best friends. I'd also grown so used to being with him that I was, I admit, rather afraid of being without him. Now in my early fifties, I'd invested the last two and a half years in our relationship, and I certainly didn't want to throw them away. Neither did he. Wasn't any long-term relationship a question of compromise and commitment? Surely, with enough effort and goodwill, we could patch up our differences and make things work — or so I frequently told myself.

The day before the Easter bank holiday, Joshua had gone away on a week's skiing trip with his school, and I planned to make the most of my freedom by spending more quality time with Zach. But, thanks to my beloved dog, the quality of this so-called quality time was turning out to be distinctly poor. The night before, I'd stayed at Zach's flat, and as I'd had no one to leave George with, naturally I'd taken him with me.

As always, George was thrilled to be going on an outing. He sat on the front seat, nose raised, peering out through the windshield at the passing houses. As soon as we arrived, he burst out of the car, charged down the long entrance hall of the Victorian mansion block where Zach lived, and then set about giving everything inside the flat a jolly good sniff. Feeling thoroughly at home, he jumped onto Zach's favorite old leather armchair and settled down for what he hoped would be a nice long nap. But what had been actively encouraged in one boy-friend's house — Alex's — was forbidden in Zach's. "No, no!" moaned my meticulous partner, as he ran over and shooed George off. "Not on the furniture!"

When we sat down to eat the special supper he'd prepared, George sat under Zach's glass-topped table, staring up at us between our plates with his headlamp eyes and whining for scraps. Then came a terrible smell: George let loose one of his signature farts.

"Phew! Oh, George!" I groaned, fanning the air.

"I'm going to throw up!" Zach mumbled from under the hand that was clamped over his nose. "That dog is unbearable. Can't you do something about him?"

"Have you any suggestions?" I sighed. "Should I stick a cork up his bum? He's only a little dog, Zach. He can't help farting!"

"Please! Do you have to be so explicit?" The F-word alone was enough to make him retch. "Put him out of the room, will you?"

"Okay. But just while we eat, darling. I can't lock him away all the time."

I shut George in Zach's extremely tidy study-cum-spare-room, expecting him to protest. Instead he was remarkably quiet. When I went back to release him ten minutes later, I discovered why. He'd wiled away the time by tipping over Zach's paper shredder, pulling out its spaghetti-thin contents, and re-shredding them. The mess was indescribable. I fell on my hands and knees and quickly stuffed the soggy mass back into the shredder before Zach saw it.

"Is everything okay?" he called from the living room.

"Fine!" I called. "Wait there — I'll be back with you in a second."

Things got worse at bedtime. Though I'd taken George's basket with me, and arranged it in a cozy corner of the study, he refused to go near it unless I was not only sitting in the room with him but actually sitting on the small sofa bed beside him. I prayed he'd settle down and go to sleep when I eventually shut the door on him, but he didn't. This resulted in a predictable and all-too-familiar row — in both senses of the word.

"What's up with that dog? Can't you make him be quiet?" Zach groaned soon after midnight as we listened to the racket coming through the partition wall behind our head.

"How can anyone *make* a dog be quiet?"

"I don't know! Put a pillow over his head!"

"That's a dreadful thing to say!"

"Why so? I've had one over *my* head for the last half hour!"

This was true. I lifted a corner of it and tried to reason with him. "Zach . . . Darling? Talk to me! Try to see this from George's point of view. Your flat is unfamiliar territory."

A muffled sigh came from under the pillow. It was closely followed by the sound of scrabbling claws in the next room. Zach sat bolt upright in bed. "Hey! What's that noise? He's scratching at the door, isn't he? He'll ruin the new paintwork!"

"Then I'll repaint it! The poor thing's scared of being alone in there overnight. He's worried that I've abandoned him."

"Oh, please! Will you stop anthropomorphizing everything that damn animal does?" Zach glared at me. If the way he'd looked at me when we first met had hit 99 out of 100 on the affection scale, his expression now would have scored minus 10.

"You know he'd stop barking if we let him in here," I said. "He'd just curl up quietly. Why are you being so difficult?"

"*I'm* being difficult?"

"Can't he sleep in here with us *just this once?* He's upset. He doesn't understand what's going on."

Zach flipped over so his back was toward

me, and pulled the pillow over his head again. "Neither do I!" His voice sounded ominous.

"What do you mean?"

"You're always making excuses for that dog!"

"No, I'm not!"

"I wish I could get away with half of what he does! Can't we have one night together without him getting in the way?"

I knew Zach was right. But that didn't stop me from feeling angry with him. Because I had a feeling that George was more than a dog to Zach, he was a symbol of my family. Why couldn't my so-called partner accept that I came as a package? Why wouldn't he embrace the rest of my life? We'd had this discussion so many times before that I knew there was no point in having it again, particularly not at this late hour.

"Let's just be practical about this, shall we?" I said matter-of-factly. "We both know that George won't stop barking unless we let him in here or I sleep in the study with him."

"Why don't you, then?"

"Okay, I will!"

So I did. George was as pleased to see me as Zach was to get rid of me. I lay down on the couch, pulled a blanket over my head, and tried to sleep, but by now George was as restless as I was upset.

When we got up later that morning, Zach and I were distinctly short with one another, so instead of spending the day with him, as I'd planned, after breakfast I put George into the car and drove back to Hampstead. I was exhausted. I needed some space and some peace and quiet. I'd forgotten that the fair was on.

Understandably, perhaps, George wasn't in my good books that day. In fact, I felt unusually annoyed with him. Of course he didn't realize. Now that he was back on home territory, he trotted around the house after me, as docile and adorable as ever. I knew I ought to take him out for a proper walk, but for once I couldn't be bothered. Even though it was a perfect spring day, I was too depressed to face the Heath with its bank holiday crowds. So when Sue, Philip, and Jessica dropped in to see me early that afternoon, I press-ganged them into taking George out for me. After the trouble he'd caused between me and Zach, I was pleased to get rid of him for half an hour.

Once they'd left for the Heath, I made myself a cup of tea and padded out into the garden in my bare feet. Though I could hear the yells, shrieks, and throbbing music coming from the fair, I sat down on the bench, closed my eyes, and let the warm sunshine wash over my face. Almost immediately the telephone rang. I rushed to answer it, hoping it might be Zach, wanting to make up with me.

It wasn't. It was my sister, calling from her mobile phone. She was sobbing, almost screaming. She sounded hysterical. "Hurry! Oh, Judith! Quick! It's terrible!"

"Sue? What on earth is it?"

"George —"

"What's he done *now?*"

"He's . . . Oh, Judith — he's been attacked!"

"What do you mean?"

"He's just been attacked! This dog — it's torn him to pieces!"

"What?"

"Please hurry! Just come! I think he's dying!"

TWENTY

The moment Sue hung up, I froze. Then I went into denial. My beautiful dog had been attacked on Hampstead Heath? He was dying? Why, that was impossible! He'd been here just five minutes ago, and he'd been perfectly fine! How could this have happened in such a short space of time? Maybe Sue was exaggerating.

But no. From the sound of her voice I could tell she hadn't been. Terrible things happened. Dogs savaged each other. Sometimes they even savaged children! I began to panic. Blood was pounding through my head in time to the beat of the reggae music coming from the fair. My George had been attacked. Aggressive dogs were a horrible, if rare, fact of life on the Heath, and since he was so defenseless he was a natural victim for them. On several occasions in the past, dogs had run up to him, sniffed him curiously, then gone for him with no provocation at all. George never snapped back — he just rolled over and gave in to them. Inevitably, aggressive dogs were accompanied by aggressive owners who started yelling at you when you tried to pull off or scare away the slavering beast that was pinning down your own helpless pup. It was only by sheer good luck that George had never been bitten. Until now.

I rushed into the house and stood in the downstairs hall, not knowing which way to turn. Suddenly my practical side kicked in. Pausing only to write down the vet's telephone number, I grabbed my keys, shoved my feet into the first pair of shoes I saw — Joshua's sneakers — and ran out of the house in the direction of the Heath. Halfway there I spotted Sue, Philip, and Jessica hurrying down the road toward me. Sue was on her phone trying to call a taxi. Jessica's face was pale and pinched. Philip was carrying George.

I looked into George's eyes. They were shocked, glazed, blank. There were puncture marks all over his hindquarters, as if someone had stabbed him repeatedly with a heavy screwdriver. Blood was pouring from his wounds, soaking into Philip's jacket and dripping onto the pavement. My dog looked as if the life was trickling out of him. He was dying in front of my eyes, and I couldn't do anything to stop it.

There was no time to talk about what had happened. We knew we had to get help — and quickly. Like Sue, I got on my phone, and with fingers shaking, dialed the vet's number. A machine answered — of course, for it was Easter Monday and the practice was closed. But the voice message gave the number of a twenty-four-hour emergency veterinary service. I tried to memorize it, but didn't quite get it, so we lost valuable time while I redialed, listened again, then dialed the next number. Then Philip spotted a taxi which, miracle of miracles, had just dropped some people off at the fair. Though George was bleeding heavily, the driver told us to get in.

As we clambered inside, someone answered my call and gave me the address of a veterinary clinic about three miles away, in Hendon. I looked at George and wondered if he'd make it there. He was dazed, plainly bewildered, and his whole body was shaking. I suddenly remembered a one-day course I'd once taken in first aid. There'd been something about shock, which could be as dangerous as a physical injury, I vaguely recalled. After an accident, it was essential to keep people warm — maybe the same applied to dogs. I took off my jacket, wrapped George in it, and while the cabbie drove us to the emergency vet in Hendon, sat on the floor, cradling him in my arms.

"What happened?" I asked.

Sue was distraught. "It was terrible. We'd literally just crossed the road onto the Heath and let him off the leash. It was very crowded on the main path so we walked toward the small wood on the left — you know, the one with the fallen tree lying across it. There were a few people sitting on it, having a picnic. They looked like — I don't know — hippies or anticapitalist demonstrators — the kind with long flowery skirts and plaits and knitted hats. The sun was shining on them through the leaves. It all looked so pretty. But as George ran ahead of us toward them this . . . this dog suddenly tore out in front of us from behind the trees."

"It came out of nowhere," Philip said. "A brown and yellow speckled bastard. A Staffordshire bull terrier. The moment it saw George it stopped in its tracks and just stood there in front of him."

"Poor darling George froze," Sue said. "I ran forward to pick him up. But before I got there this creature went for him! It just sank its teeth into him and started shaking him, as if George was some kind of doll."

"Mummy was very brave," Jessica said. "She ran up and hit the dog with her handbag. But it wouldn't let go . . ."

"One of the women sitting on the fallen tree ran over and started screaming at the Staffordshire, too. It turned out she was its owner. She tried to pull it off, but she couldn't. Not only wasn't it on a leash, it wasn't even wearing a collar! It was completely out of control! So she started hitting it over the head."

"And then all these other people came running up, people who had nothing to do with it, and shouted at her to stop beating her dog, even though it was still attacking George!"

"I thought, that's it — it's going to kill him!" Sue sobbed.

"And then it suddenly let go of George."

"Philip carried George away, and bumped into one of the Heath constables. And the policeman came running over to me. I was still shouting at the woman."

"He told her to stop beating the dog. And he's taken her details. He says he's going to prosecute." Sue wiped the tears from her face. "I'm so, so sorry!"

"Why? It wasn't your fault!"

"If we hadn't taken George for a walk this

wouldn't have happened!"

"I *asked* you to take him! I *wanted* him out of the house! If anyone's to blame it's me!"

By this time, we'd arrived at the emergency veterinary practice on Hendon Way. Sue, Jessica, and I ran in with George while Philip paid the taxi driver; even though the doors of his cab were smeared with blood, he refused to accept a tip. Inside, a nurse took George from me and rushed him through to the vet, leaving us in the reception area for what seemed like hours. Jessica threw her arms around me, but I was beyond being comforted. I knew that George was only a dog, not a human being, but I still couldn't bear the thought that I was about to lose him.

Eventually the vet called me into his consulting room. George wasn't there — he was being looked after in the ward at the back, he reassured me when he saw the alarmed look on my face. George appeared to be seriously injured, he told me, and he was also in shock.

"Shock is the body's response to trauma," he explained. "We humans have it, too. The two most vital organs in the body are the brain and the heart, and in order to preserve them in times of trauma, and to make sure they get enough oxygen, the blood supply to all the other organs — the liver, the kidneys, the bowels, and the skin, for instance — gets cut off. The body kind of shuts itself down, if you like. It's a self-defense mechanism."

"So isn't that good?"

"Yes and no. The problem arises if the other organs are starved of oxygen for too long. If that happens, they might go into shock as well. And that is very dangerous. It sets off other problems — liver or kidney failure, for instance. But we don't know that's going to happen. Look, it's touch-and-go at the moment. We've given your dog strong painkillers and put him on an intravenous drip to increase the volume of his blood and to try to make sure that his organs get enough oxygen. Once we've stabilized him, we'll be able to operate and clean his wounds. From what we can see, he's received multiple lacerations to his left hind leg, but we don't yet know what's going on inside him. There could be internal bleeding."

I nodded numbly. I could scarcely take it all in.

"You might as well go home," he told me gently. "We'll call you as soon as we have any news."

"Would it be possible for me to see George first?"

While I followed him down a short corridor, the vet told me that George was the second dog that day who'd been brought in after being attacked by a Staffordshire bull terrier on Hampstead Heath, and the aggressor might have been the same crazy animal.

We pushed through a door into a spotlessly clean ward straight out of *ER*, where two or three nurses were working in green overalls. A bank of spotlights hung above a big steel bench near us — it looked like an operating table — and a wall at one end of the room was made up of a floor-to-ceiling stack of mesh-fronted cages or pens. There were only two animals in them. One was a Jack Russell — the first dog to have been attacked that afternoon. The other was George.

Like the Jack Russell, George was lying in a small pen with an open door. He seemed to be struggling to keep his head raised, but it was lolling sideways. His mouth hung open, and he was panting — short, quick, shallow breaths. One of his paws had been partially shaved and attached to a cannula, and there was an intravenous drip going into it. Several pressure pads had been placed over his injuries, and blood was seeping through them. He looked like the victim of a car accident.

I stroked his muzzle, which was caked with dried blood. When he realized it was me, he became restless and attempted to stand up, but immediately collapsed on his injured haunches with a moan. His eyes gazed numbly up into mine. He clearly hadn't a clue why he was in pain, or what was happening to him, and I couldn't explain any of it to him. I felt helpless. All I could say was "You'll be all right, George. I promise. You've got to be."

I didn't want to leave him, but I could hardly sit on the floor beside him all night long, getting under the nurses' feet. I'd only be a hindrance. Besides, as everyone there clearly knew what they were doing, I felt that George was in the best possible hands.

It was time to go. I put my head inside the cage and kissed the soft, downy fluff on top of George's head. Then I stood up and walked out of the door. I had no idea if I'd ever see him alive again.

Twenty-One

Back home, I let myself into the empty house and threw myself down on the red velvet sofa, next to the small dip in the cushions George's body had made just hours before.

Except for the background noise of the fair, the house sang with silence. There was no soft, piglike grunting to be heard. No deep sighs. No snoring. No regular breathing, save my own. No barking, yelping, or whining for food. No slam of the newly enlarged cat flap as George squeezed out into the garden in pursuit of a trespassing pigeon or cat. No shredding of paper tissues. No pitter-patter of claws across the wooden floor.

I thought of the joy he'd brought into the house in the years since we'd had him. Was this to be the end of it? A dreadful thought was running through the back of my mind like a piece of ticker tape: if George died,

I'd have to break the news to Joshua when he came home from his skiing trip. What a great homecoming that would be. I remembered the dreadful morning almost seven years before when I'd had to tell him his father had died. Nothing could be worse than that moment. George was only a dog, I told myself repeatedly. Still, it wasn't fair that my son should have to deal with death again.

Downstairs, the house seemed even quieter. George's basket lay on the floor of my study, empty but for a half-eaten dog biscuit peeping out of the folds of the blanket. At the sight of it my tears welled up again and so, too, did my anger. And like the Staffordshire bull terrier, I needed a victim on which to vent my aggression.

I picked up the telephone and dialed Zach's number. He answered with a curt "Hello?"

"George has been attacked," I said accusingly.

"What are you talking about?"

"George was attacked, Zach. On the Heath."

"Oh?" He sounded bored. He wasn't taking me seriously.

"By a mad dog! He's in an animal hospital, Zach! He might die!"

At last he heard me. "But that's appalling! Where are you?"

"At home!" I shouted.

"Wait there. I'm on my way."

"I bet you'd be pleased if George didn't survive!" I berated him, when he arrived forty minutes later to find me red-eyed and surrounded by a pile of sopping wet tissues that might have been mangled by my dog.

He looked horrified. "How can you say such a thing? It's so unfair. You must think I'm a monster."

"Yes! I do! You hate George!"

Zach smiled somewhat sadly and blotted my tearful face. "Look, darling, I may not love him as you do, but I don't hate him. And I'd never want any harm to come to him."

As the vet discovered when he operated the following morning, George had sustained extremely serious injuries during the ferocious attack. With his powerful jaws and sharklike teeth, the Staffordshire bull terrier had crunched through George's left hind leg and haunches seven times, slashing through the veins, shredding the muscles as he shook him, and gouging lumps out of his flesh, leaving gaping cavities inside George's body to which the vet referred graphically as "dead space." Though the beast's teeth had narrowly missed George's vital organs, it was likely that they'd introduced thousands of harmful bacteria into his bloodstream and tissues. Although George had survived the trauma, we had yet to see if those organisms, and his injuries, would cause a fatal infection. He was still in danger.

When I telephoned that evening, the practice staff told me that George was doing as well as could be expected. I spent the night on tenterhooks, then called again the following morning, and was told that his progress was still good. By that evening he'd miraculously staggered to his feet, and I was told that, if he continued to make such good progress, I could take him home tomorrow.

Scarcely able to believe our luck, Sue and I went together to pick George up. His left hind leg was a mass of stitches and bandages, and there were two or three long thin plastic tubes called Penrose drains sticking out of his haunches at odd angles to drain the fluid from his wounds, giving him the somewhat peculiar appearance of a drinking-straw dispenser. Bruised, battered, swollen, on antibiotics, and on methadone for the pain, George wasn't yet out of the woods, but he was on his way. Who would have expected our pajama case to be such a trouper?

Though he couldn't yet wag his tail or walk more than a couple of steps, I could tell from George's eyes that he was pleased to be home. When friends and family came to visit him, as they did in great numbers, he limped slowly and painfully up to them, dragging his injured leg. A brown, sticky, bloody liquid oozed constantly from his plastic drains and dripped all over the carpets. I didn't care how much mess it made. I'd clean the place up when he was better.

The bill for the exemplary treatment he'd received at the emergency veterinary office came to just under a thousand pounds. I'd gladly have paid double. I felt like a prisoner who'd been granted a reprieve from a life sentence. Feeling guilty that I'd been annoyed with him just before he was attacked, I became George's devoted nurse and slave. So what was new? Squeamish as I am, I administered drugs and painkillers, changed bandages, and swabbed the weeping holes from whence the drains emerged. I poached chicken breasts and boiled bowlfuls of rice for him, invalid food which, because he had little appetite, I fed to him by hand. Because he couldn't manage the stairs, I carried him carefully up and down them every time I moved around the house, and I didn't even flinch when his drains wept all over my clothes. Since he wasn't able to jump onto the sofas, I made George a comfortable bed of cushions by the living room fireplace, another in the kitchen, and another in my study. I also moved his basket into my bedroom so that he could sleep close to me at night.

To my amazement Zach didn't kick up a fuss about it. He accepted that George was too ill to sleep alone and, earplugs in, heroically put up with the sighs, snorts, snores, and snuffles that came from his basket. While I looked after my Cavalier, Zach looked after me. I was beginning to think we'd turned a corner and that my somewhat detached partner was at last shaking off his dog phobia. Perhaps he was even becoming a family man at last.

When Joshua came home from his skiing trip the following weekend, George still had the drinking straws sticking out of him, and he was still limping badly, as he would continue to do for another six months. But, as I reassured my distressed son, our dog was definitely on the road to recovery.

George would never be quite the same again. The Staffordshire had inflicted permanent damage to his nervous system. From now on his legs would tremble uncontrollably at times, even when he was sitting down. The experience of being attacked had sapped both his immune system and his confidence. It had aged George. Psychologically, he was a mess — nervous, insecure, and clingy. He couldn't bear to be parted from me for a second. He dogged my every footstep while I was cooking in the kitchen. He sat close beside my chair while I worked, staring up at me for hours, and if I didn't look at him every few minutes, he barked until I did. If I so much as stood up, George struggled to his feet in case I was leaving him. He waited outside the bathroom whenever I went in, and if I didn't come out within an allotted thirty-second span, he yelped and scrabbled at the door. No sooner had I sat down on the sofa than he was on my lap or, since jumping was still difficult for him, pawing my knees to be picked up.

At first I was flattered by these persistent demands for attention — it's always nice to feel that someone can't live without you — but within a few months I began to feel suffocated. George now kept a tab on my whereabouts at all times. I couldn't move without him following me, and if I had to go out without him, he sat at the window, staring out into the street, and waiting for me to return.

George had become overdependent on me, not to say overpossessive. He'd changed from being an affectionate but bossy king into a jealous dictator. Gone were the days when it had been Joshua who'd tried to see off a male companion. This was now George's province. My life had turned into a second Shakespearian drama. *Hamlet, Prince of Denmark* was over, but *Othello* was now playing, and George had taken the starring role and cast Zach as Cassio, the focus of his jealousy. On evenings when my partner came over to the house, George greeted him with an icy stare. He pushed reproachfully between us when we sat next to each other on the sofa, poked his head suspiciously around the door of any room we happened to be in, and barked like a maniac if Zach tried to kiss me. Even I knew that it was time for a few canine boundaries to be drawn.

"Look, this is too much," Zach snapped one Sunday morning as George sat beside the bed, growling softly but insistently at him as he tried to read the papers.

I threw down my own newspaper. "I know," I admitted. "Stop that, George!" My dog ignored me. "Stop it! Come HERE!

Oh, it's hopeless! The thing is, darling, he knows you don't like him."

"So it's my fault he's badly behaved? Please!"

"What are we going to do about him?"

Zach threw down his newspaper and glared at me. "More to the point, what are *you* going to do about him? What do I know about training dogs?"

"Well, I don't seem to know much either, do I?"

"I thought you were an expert."

"Thank you," I said curtly. "There's something wrong here, isn't there?"

"Ah, at last you've seen the light!"

"I mean, perhaps George is lonely. Perhaps if I got another little dog as well, a sort of friend and companion for him, he wouldn't be so clingy?"

"Another little dog?" My partner looked at me as if I were an alien. "That's a great idea. Brilliant, Judith. Why don't you look for another little *man* at the same time?"

"Maybe I will!"

Zach shook his head "Look, I know George was attacked, but he's better now. And he's ruling your life and Joshua's. And ruining mine! He's got you under his paw. I simply can't bear it anymore."

I burst into tears. "Leave me, then, if

that's what you want!"

He smiled, rather sadly, and stroked my cheek. "I *don't* want. That's my problem. But you have to face facts. Our relationship is untenable at the moment. Sometimes I think I come last on your list of priorities. I certainly come after this mutt. And that's *your* problem. You need to deal with it. Maybe you should take him back to the vet. You seem to live there anyway. Perhaps you *should* live there."

"What? With Greg?"

Zach shrugged. "He'd be perfect for you. After all, he's an animal lover. And you'd save on gas, and you wouldn't have to pay his astronomical bills."

Twenty-Two

Greg took one look at my distraught face and the shadows under my eyes and said, "If you ask me, this is a clear case of post-traumatic stress disorder."

I knew I'd been feeling down and unable to cope in the months since George's attack, but I hadn't been able to put my finger on what was wrong with me. Now at long last someone had. I felt so relieved I wanted to hug him. Perhaps Zach had been right — I should go out with him. "Thank you *so* much," I sighed, holding back the tears. "The whole attack thing's thrown up a lot of issues for me — a lot of feelings I buried after my husband died. About grief. And loss. George being attacked has brought everything flooding back. I can't sleep properly, and I'm tearful all the time. I thought I could cope, but it turns out I can't. Do you think I should see my doctor?"

He cleared his throat. "Actually I meant George. He's the one suffering from post-traumatic stress disorder. The attack has obviously had a profound effect on him. I recommend you call in a pet behaviorist." He handed me a card. "Try Janine Grey," he said, and all but thrust me out of the door. "She'll set you on the right track."

Janine Grey, MSc, animal psychologist and pet behaviorist, breezed into my home two days later with the same brisk air of authority with which my old headmistress, Miss Kynaston, had once swept into the school hall for morning assembly. But while Miss Kynaston had been a frosty gorgon with a pinched mouth, a tight white perm, and cold blue eyes — a single stare from which could reduce the most impudent schoolgirl to a trembling wreck — Janine was young and very pretty, with long brown hair and big brown eyes. She emanated good sense and warmth.

Used to being made a big fuss of by everyone who came to the house, George immediately limped up to our new visitor, who, as everyone else did, crouched to greet him. "Hello, George!" she said cheerily, giving his ears a good rub. "I hear you've been in the wars." In answer, George put his front paws onto her bent knees and aimed his tongue at her face — his usual manner of greeting. "Now, stop that," said Janine, in her genial but firm voice.

"Fat chance." I laughed. "Licking people is an obsession of his! George never stops!"

"Well, it's not nice, is it, George?" said Janine firmly. "You're going to stop, aren't you? That's enough now!" To my amazement, George's tongue slid back into his mouth and stayed there. "Good boy!" Janine stood up and pointed to the corner of the kitchen. "Now, go and sit down over there," she said. "Your owner and I need to talk." Tail wagging, George limped obediently to the corner and lay on the floor, his nose between his paws. "Good boy!" said Janine again. She sat down at the table and motioned for me to do the same. I did so. She flashed me a smile. "So what's the problem?"

"Well . . ." I glanced at the well-behaved fluffball, lying in the corner like a peaceful angel. "Basically, um, George has become uncontrollable. He won't do as he's told."

"Really?" Janine said, with an upward, questioning lilt to her voice.

"You see, as I explained on the telephone, he was attacked and nearly killed a few months ago."

"Nearly killed?" she repeated.

"And ever since then, well, he's been insecure and needy."

"Needy?" she echoed.

"Yes. Much more so than usual. He's incredibly clingy. I understand why, of course. He's been in pain, and the poor thing's probably still traumatized by what happened to him. He can't bear to be without me. Even for a minute."

Janine Grey nodded. "*He* can't bear it? Not for a minute? Is that right?"

"Yes, it is. I can scarcely go out without him. He makes such a fuss that I have to take him with me. And sometimes it's just not practical. And I'm with him nearly all the time! But whenever I'm not looking at him, he tries to attract my attention. The nights are the worst."

"The nights?"

"Yes. George barks nonstop. And he wants to go out for a pee at three or four in the morning. He wakes everyone up. Including my son Joshua and Zach."

"And is he — Zach — your son's father?"

"No. My husband died years ago. Zach's my boyfriend. Well, more of a man-friend. He's fifty-seven. Anyway, George is making a lot of trouble between us."

"Trouble? *George* is?" Janine blinked at me.

"Well, yes. He wants to be in the bedroom with us."

"In the bedroom?"

"Actually, he'd like to be on the bed. I wouldn't mind, but my partner — Zach — he can't stand him being there."

"He can't?"

"He's not what you'd call a doggie person. Or a family man, for that matter."

"*Not* a family man? Is that right?"

Yes, it damn well was right. By now I was beginning to feel a little impatient, not to say uneasy, about the direction we were going in. Janine Grey was charging a whopping £140 for her two-hour consultation. That was a bloody fortune — more than double the hourly rate that Udi had charged his psychotherapy clients for their sessions, and they'd been human. Was she going to echo everything I said for the entire one hundred and twenty minutes? "It's absolutely right," I went on rather forcefully. "He may seem calm now, but that's because he's sleeping, isn't he? But believe me, Zach's really very difficult and possessive. Sometimes I feel I can't cope with him anymore."

Janine raised her perfectly arched eyebrows. "*Zach* is difficult?" she repeated. "You can't cope with *him?*"

"Yes, he's . . ."

x

309

"*Zach* is very difficult?"

I looked at the pet behaviorist as if she were mad. "Sorry? Why do you say that?"

"I didn't say it, Judith. You did. You said, 'Zach's very difficult and possessive. Sometimes I feel I can't cope with him anymore.'"

"Did I? Are you sure? Oh, well, it must have been a slip of the tongue. I meant George, of course. He's driving Zach mad. And me, too."

Janine glanced over her shoulder at the docile dog lying in the corner. I did the same. George had one eye open. And the moment he saw me looking at him, he yapped.

"See, there he goes now! I told you! Stop it, George!" Still yapping, he got up, limped over to me, and started scrabbling at my knees for me to pick him up. I pushed him off. "Go away, darling!"

"Take your eyes off him, Judith," Janine said quietly.

"I'm sorry?"

"Break eye contact. Now. Right now. That's good. Well done. You see, if you look at George when he barks, you're only reinforcing his need for attention. And if you keep talking to him when he does something you don't like, it's counterproductive. You're rewarding his demanding behavior. That only encourages him to do it again. See? He's stopped barking now."

George had given up trying to get onto my lap, too. He limped over to the sofa and, with difficulty, jumped onto it. Something stirred in my memory. "Reward good behavior," I muttered. "Ignore the bad." Over the years this had become one of Joshua's favorite mantras, especially when he'd done something wrong himself.

Janine smiled. "You've been to dog training classes."

"I consulted a trainer. Once. It was a long time ago."

"And how did you get on with the training?"

"I, um . . . Oh, well, I gave up."

"Right!" This time there was no question mark at the end of her word. My headmistress came flashing back into my mind, and the clipped, disapproving way she'd spoken to me when I'd been caught absentmindedly carving the words "I love the Beatles" with the point of my compasses on a desk in the chemistry lab.

I smiled sheepishly. "I guess it wasn't a good idea to give up, was it?"

"I guess not."

"Oh dear! Would you like a cup of tea or

coffee? And would you like to examine George now?"

"Examine him?" We both gazed at the dog now conked out on the sofa. "Let's let sleeping dogs lie for a bit, shall we? I think it would be more useful if we carried on talking about you."

"Me?"

She nodded. "And your family. Zach, for example."

"Zach? What's he got to do with George?"

Janine smiled, and put her hand over mine. "Don't take this the wrong way, Judith, but in my experience, dogs are sensitive creatures. They pick up on their owners' feelings very quickly. They know if something's wrong. Tension in the air at home — that sort of thing. Look, I can suggest all sorts of tricks that might help calm George down — putting a pheromone diffuser in the room where he sleeps, for instance — and I'll give you lots of tips about how best to manage him . . ."

"That's what I want!"

"But you are his owner. And, as such, you're responsible for how he behaves. Your happiness affects him. If you're insecure or unhappy, for instance, he will be, too. So I can't help wondering if he's not the only one who needs sorting out here."

Twenty-Three

It was another Sunday, and one of those glorious Indian summer mornings you only get at the very beginning of October. The air was balmy, and the sunlight had a special quality: everything it touched — the houses, the trees, the bumblebees, the weeds that were running riot in my garden — looked as if it had been dipped in liquid gold.

Inside my flat, though, the conversation appeared to be dripping with acid. Thanks to George's shenanigans, Zach and I had had another broken night, and we were already at each other's throats.

"Let's get out of here," my partner snapped as we sat at the kitchen table, trying to revive ourselves with copious amounts of strong coffee. "Why don't we drive out to the countryside and take a walk?"

"Okay," I said. And added, after a short pause, "Perhaps I'll ask Joshua if he'd like to come with us."

"Joshua?" Something about the way my partner said my son's name grated on my nerves. "He's still sleeping, isn't he?"

"I can always wake him up."

"Give the guy a break, Judith. It's Sunday morning. You know he won't want to come. I'm sure he'd much rather stay in London, hanging out down at Camden market, or playing poker and behaving disreputably with his friends."

"That's what I'm afraid of."

"Besides, walking isn't Joshua's thing. He'd be bored."

"It'd do him good to be out in the fresh air for once, Zach, instead of breathing in pollution or sitting slumped in front of a computer."

"And what healthy teenager wants to do anything that's good for him? Besides," he added, with an edge to his voice, "you and I haven't spent much time together lately. Is it too much to want you to myself for one day?"

I should have felt flattered that Zach wanted to be alone with me. Instead, I felt claustrophobic. I finished my coffee. "What about George, then?" I said, after a short pause.

"What about him?"

"Well, if we're going for a walk in the

countryside surely we can take *him* with us?"

Zach gave a long-suffering sigh. "We'll want to have lunch somewhere. And he won't be allowed in. And he may — you know — in the car."

"We'll keep the windows open. I'm sure you can put up with it for once," I said, rather icily. Obviously he couldn't, because a frosty silence blasted back at me across the table. "Zach?"

"Look, I want to do some proper walking. A good few miles. I really need the exercise. That's too much for George, with his injured leg. He'll get tired."

"Then I'll have to take him for a walk before we go." Now it was my turn to sigh. I knew that Zach was right in what he had said, but it still rankled. I started to speak, then stopped myself. What was the point when it would only provoke an argument? Zach and I had had more than enough of those lately. But what the hell? One more row was but a drop in the ocean. "Zach, surely the whole point of us having a day out is that we both enjoy ourselves?"

"Naturally."

"But I won't enjoy walking in the country-side if I know that Joshua's all alone in London and George is shut up here."

"He's a *dog!*"

"Precisely!"

"Look, if he comes with us, we might as well not go."

"Fine! Let's not, then!"

Eventually we reached one of the many compromises we were finding it increasingly difficult to come to. Zach would set off by himself for a long walk on the Heath. It wasn't the same as the countryside, he said begrudgingly, but he supposed it was better than nothing. Meanwhile I'd make up a picnic and walk across to join him at Kenwood House, bringing George with me.

Once Zach had left, taking his bad mood with him, I felt a sense of relief. I put the radio on and bustled around the kitchen. While I stood at the counter slicing bread for sandwiches, with far more force than was necessary, George skated around my feet, and snaffled up any crumbs that fell.

"Morning!" said Joshua, cheerfully, appearing at the door in his dressing gown. "What are you doing?"

"Walking across the Heath and having a picnic at Kenwood with Zach. Do you want to come?"

My son looked horrified. "A walk? It's Sunday — my day of rest!"

So Zach had been right. How annoying! As his mother had once told me, not without

316

irony, when we'd talked on the telephone, the men in the O'Neill family were always right.

I set off across the Heath with George trotting beside me on the extendable leash, wagging his tail. The beautiful weather had brought out crowds of people. There were parents with small children feeding the ducks and swans on the pond in the Vale of Health, lone dog walkers such as myself, and elderly couples strolling arm in arm. I looked at them enviously and with awe: how *did* couples manage to grow old together nowadays, when staying together was so hard?

Two men were coming down the path in my direction, absorbed in an animated conversation. One was in his mid-fifties — about the age Udi had been when he'd died. His companion, who shared many of his features, was in his late teens or early twenties. It was obvious to me that they were father and son. As they passed me, I heard them laugh together, as if at some private joke. A great sadness overwhelmed me.

Feeling tearful, I cut off the path and through a clearing, where there were fewer people about. There was a heavy weight on my shoulders — and it wasn't the backpack of food strapped to me. I remembered with what joy I'd always left home to meet Zach when we'd first met, just over three years before. Then, I couldn't wait to see him. I'd had such high hopes for our future that I'd smiled all the way. And now? Recently I'd found myself unable to smile much at all, and certainly not when he was around.

I thought suddenly of Janine Grey. Ever since the pet behaviorist had left my house a few months before, leaving me emotionally spent and conked out on the couch next to my dog, I'd been trying to blot out what she'd talked to me about. It wasn't only George who needed sorting out, she'd more than hinted, it was me, or rather my relationship with Zach. It may have possessed some diamond qualities, but, like all but the most perfect of diamonds, it had a flaw. I had to face facts: as much as we loved each other, and got on brilliantly when we were alone in our bubble, our relationship didn't work in the real world.

Time and again Zach and I had brushed our differences under the carpet. But after three years, the pile there had grown to the size of an adult Saint Bernard. Lately it had become impossible to ignore. We tripped over it every time we stepped out together. We'd started to resent one another. And it was horrible.

The path through the woods was bordered by a maze of fenced-off areas containing tall trees, fallen mossy tree trunks, and thick undergrowth. There must have been hundreds of rabbits and squirrels living there, and no doubt many foxes, for George had his nose to the ground the whole time and was sniffing excitedly, wagging his tail at double-time, and straining at the end of his leash. Soon I glimpsed the front of Kenwood House through the branches. My spirits lifted, as they always did when I saw it. The former stately home was a masterpiece designed by the eighteenth-century architect Robert Adam, who'd remodeled an older house on the site for William Murray, 1st earl of Mansfield, a British politician and judge who had played an important role in the abolition of slavery in Britain: his landmark "Somerset ruling" of 1772, over the fate of runaway slave James Somerset, had declared that no slave could be forcibly removed from Britain by his master and sold abroad.

Robert Adam had created a veritable confection of a mansion for Mansfield. Built on top of a hill on the northern perimeter of Hampstead Heath, the classically inspired building was covered with blindingly white stucco and resembled a long, low wedding cake iced with elaborate designs. Left to the nation in 1927 by a subsequent owner, the brewing magnate Edward Cecil Guinness, it was now a museum full of priceless paintings and was often used as a movie set, most famously in *Notting Hill,* where it was the backdrop to a scene between Hugh Grant and Julia Roberts.

I walked past the small lake with its trompe l'oeil bridge, and up the grassy hill upon which the house was perched. Zach was waiting for me on the upper slopes. He smiled at me so warmly that I felt a surge of love for him. Our differences weren't his fault, I told myself. Well, not *all* his fault! He couldn't help not wanting the same things in life that I did. But by the time we'd spread out the rug he'd carried over and unpacked the picnic, the moment had passed. We were back at each other's throats, and what had been an exquisitely blue sky above us was clouding over. George didn't notice. He was too intent on finding out what was inside the sandwiches I'd brought.

"Get him off, can't you?" Zach cried, as my pooch trampled across the rug to claim a fallen sliver of chicken.

I did my best, in the interest of peace as well as hygiene. "Off, George! Now, sit! Down! There's a good boy!" And with the aid of a little bribery — half the contents of my own sandwich — George obeyed me. Until the food ran out, that was.

We opened the Sunday papers and tried to read them. I say "tried" because every time I opened the pages, George head-butted underneath them or trampled over them. Zach sighed. Since there were few dogs about, I eventually let George off the leash. I knew he wouldn't stray far from me — he never did nowadays. Ever since he'd been attacked, he'd been terrified of other dogs, and froze whenever he saw one. But when he spotted another Cavalier frolicking down by the lake, his ears pricked up and he ran down the hill to greet it. Like the rest of his breed, George was able to recognize one of his own, and always said hello to it.

"I'd better go after him," I said. "He's not even meant to be off the leash here."

"Don't fuss after him," said Zach. "Why don't you give yourself a break and read the papers while we've got some peace?"

I settled down to read, glancing up every now and then to look at George, who was beside the lake, near the entrance to the woods through which we'd walked earlier. By now the clouds had gathered thickly overhead and blotted out the sun. A wind was blowing up. I shivered. "I think it's going to rain," I said.

"Something else for you to worry about," Zach muttered. I gritted my teeth.

And then it did rain — suddenly and with the same monsoon force it had on the day three years before when Zach and I had first met at the St. George's Hotel. We jumped to our feet, as did all the other people sitting on the grass, and started shoving the remains of our picnic, and the scattering newspapers, into our bags. I looked down the hill toward the lake, but I couldn't see George there. In fact, I couldn't see him anywhere.

"Where's George?" I said, as I peered into the distance. "Zach, I can't see him!"

"He must be somewhere. Hey, help me pack up this stuff, will you? Quick! I'm getting drenched!"

"But where is he?" Everyone around us was running up to the house for shelter, so by now the lower slopes of the hill were almost deserted. There was no sign of George. As I gathered up the sodden newspapers, which were blowing all over the grass, I called his name repeatedly, but my voice was drowned by the rain. As the dry earth turned to mud under our feet, Zach picked up the bags and scrabbled up the hill to the gravel path.

"Come on, Judith!" he called. "He'll turn up!"

"I've got to find him!"

I cursed myself for ever taking my eyes off my dog. Why had I been so stupid as to let him off the leash? Suddenly I remembered the eagerness with which he'd sniffed his way through the woods en route to Kenwood. "I bet he's run into the woods. I know we'll find him there!"

Zach had taken shelter under an ivy-clad archway. "We?" he called. "No. He'll find his way home!"

"No, he won't." I scrambled up the bank to join him. By now we were the only people still there. "He's not that kind of dog! He'll get eaten by a fox! He'll — he'll find a road and get run over! He will! You know he will. Like the vet said, stuff happens to George!"

Zach shook his head in despair. His clothes, like mine, were plastered to his body. "I can't stand this. I'm going into the house before I drown," he said, "and I suggest you do the same. I'll help you find that bloody animal when it's stopped raining."

"I'm going to look for him now."

"Suit yourself."

"You could come and help me."

"I told you, I'll come when it stops raining."

"But that might be too late!"

We glared at each other. Suddenly a lot more seemed to be at stake than George's safety. I took Zach's hand. "Please come with me!"

He pulled his hand free and picked up the bags. "George can look after himself for once. He's only a dog, Judith! Not that anyone would know it, the way you treat him!"

"He may be only a dog to you, but he's part of my family."

"And I'm not?"

The rain beat on my head and shoulders. It beat on the gravel around us, like a drum tattoo.

"You don't want to be," I said, above the noise. "You never have, have you?" Zach said nothing. "Look, I've got to go. George is important to me."

"More important than I am."

What was the point in replying? "I'll see you later."

"Perhaps."

I turned away and ran down the slippery grass toward the woods. Halfway down, I stopped and looked back toward the house, in the hope that Zach might have followed me. He was still standing under the ivy archway with his wet white shirt clinging to him. I signaled for him to come and join me. But he stayed where he was.

I thought suddenly of these perfect jeans to which I'd once likened our relationship. During the past few months the zip had broken and the waistline had been held together by a large safety-pin. I'd scarcely been able to breathe in them. This time they were beyond repair. I stepped out of them and ran toward the woods in pursuit of George.

Zach was right about George managing to find his way home. Mind you, George didn't actually get back there under his own steam. He *was* lost, and wandering around aimlessly on the Heath, and when the rain bucketed down with such force, he ran up to a woman who was sheltering under a tree. When she realized that no one was with him, she used her mobile phone to call my mobile phone number, which was engraved on the identity disk on his collar. Since she and I were unable to find each other on the Heath, she volunteered to take George back to her car and then drop him off at our place.

Half an hour later, an extremely happy Cavalier was chauffeured to our house by

Porsche, where Joshua took him in and gratefully thanked the woman.

Meanwhile, I walked home in the pouring rain. By myself.

It took my son a week to notice that my partner of three and a half years' standing was no longer around.

"Where's Zach?" he asked, late one night, as we lounged on the sofas, watching television together. *Desperate Housewives* was just coming to an end, and the divorced Susan was quarreling with her boyfriend, Mike Delfino. I can't imagine why that had made Joshua think of Zach.

"I've no idea," I said.

Joshua narrowed his eyes suspiciously. "Have you two split up?"

"Yes, we most certainly have."

"When?"

"Last Sunday."

"You didn't tell me!"

"Maybe I didn't want to talk about it."

"Are you okay about it, Mum?"

"Absolutely," I said with more certainty than I felt. "It's what I want."

"Oh. That's all right then." Joshua turned back to the television, where another character — the gorgeous Gabrielle — was walking down Wisteria Drive in a skimpy red gown. "It's a shame, though," he said.

I looked at him in astonishment. "What do you mean? Are you sorry?"

"Yes."

"You mean you actually *like* Zach?"

"Yeah. He's okay."

"Okay? What does that mean? Turn the volume down, Joshua! Don't look at Gabrielle, look at me! Can you unpack that a little?"

I stared at my son as he lay sprawled on the other sofa, his socked feet sticking over the far arm and the sleeping George stretched across his lap. Perhaps I hadn't looked at him properly for a while: I suddenly noticed how incredibly long his legs were and, when he turned toward me again, how handsome and grown-up his face had become.

"Well, Zach's a bit dry, of course," he said. "He can't stand loud music. And he always complains when the television's on. On the other hand he can play poker. And he knows good jokes. And he's not in my face all the time. And he tells you to stop fussing over me and nagging me to eat vegetables and stupid stuff like that, which is a very big plus. Of course I like him. But it's your life, Mum," he added, easing George carefully off his lap. "Whatever makes you happy."

And, having dropped this bombshell, my six-foot-tall sixteen-year-old son stood up, patted my shoulder as if I were an elderly invalid he had to humor, then went downstairs to his bedroom, shut the door behind him, and got on with his own life. I was flabbergasted.

At least someone in the house was genuinely pleased to see the back of Zach. He had snuck into my bedroom on the night we'd split up, and settled down to sleep at the end of my bed: a fluffy chestnut-and-white pajama case of a dog with a beatific smile on his face.

As well he might have. His persistence had paid off. George now had me all to himself again. As usual, the King of the Canines had got his way.

Twenty-Four

Recently I took George to have his annual medical checkup. Kirstie, a relatively new young vet at the practice, took his temperature with her disgusting rectal thermometer, peered into his ears with a light, pressed his rotund tummy with her fingers, then deposited him on the scales. Although George had been on a strict diet for the last six months, my formerly anorexic pooch weighed in at a hefty 11.50 kilos, which was at least one and a half more than the top limit for his breed.

At the end of the examination, Kirstie listened to George's chest with her stethoscope. "Even though he's a little bit overweight, he seems to be in very good health," she said afterward, "apart from his heart murmur."

"But George doesn't have a heart murmur!" I exclaimed.

Kirstie listened to his chest again, then

looked at me sympathetically through big, round, blue eyes. "I'm very sorry to tell you, but he does."

I caught my breath. Of all the many ailments that George had suffered from over the years, heart disease had never been among them. Unlike many Cavaliers' hearts, his had always been in perfect condition. Or so I'd thought.

"I'm afraid it's probably mitral valve disease," Kirstie added.

I nodded. I'd heard of the dreaded MVD, as it was called for short, but knew little about it. As Kirstie now explained to me, as tactfully as possible, it was a serious, degenerative, and life-shortening condition of the heart's mitral valve, a set of double flaps that operated like one-way doors to keep blood flowing through the heart in one direction. As the blood passed from the left atrium into the left ventricle, the mitral valve prevented it flowing backward. In MVD, the valve gradually lost its flexibility and it no longer closed properly. Consequently, as the heart beat or contracted, blood was pushed back up into the atrium, which produced the murmuring sound she could hear through her stethoscope. As the condition worsened, the atrium and the ventricle enlarged, and this in turn affected the lungs. If and when the condition got really bad, the mitral valve could collapse, causing immediate cardiac arrest — and death.

Humans could get MVD, and apparently so could all dogs. The disease, however, was a whopping twenty-one times more prevalent in Cavalier King Charles Spaniels than in other breeds. More than half of Cavaliers over the age of five had been found to have it, and it affected practically every Cavalier above the age of ten. It probably had something to do with all that royal inbreeding.

In the past I'd always counted myself lucky that George's heart was clear. Not anymore, though. The blood was whooshing backward through his heart like water backing up in a drain. On a seriousness scale of one to six, Kirstie rated the murmur at three. Maybe no one had noticed it before, she suggested. That was impossible, I said: her predecessors at the practice had listened to George's heart countless times over the past eight years, and they'd always been impressed that it was murmur-free. This must be something new. Had I detected a decrease in George's physical activity in recent months? she asked, for that was another symptom of developing MVD. A decrease in his physical activity? I burst out laughing. What physical activity? George had always spent a good three-quarters of his life asleep.

Outside, I opened the back door of the car. "On the backseat, George!" I ordered him. He jumped in and obediently took his designated place. But by the time I'd got behind the wheel, he'd squeezed through the narrow gap between the front seats, clambered over the hand brake, and was occupying the front passenger seat next to me, as per usual. Delighted to be in the car — four wheels rather than four legs always his preferred method of getting from A to B — he sat beside me as I drove home, exactly as he'd done for more than eight years, his body erect and his little black nose raised so that he could peer out through the windshield. I glanced at him surreptitiously and, when I pulled up at the traffic light, reached over and gave his right ear a good scratch. George turned toward me, looked into my eyes, and gave a deep, contented sigh. Suddenly there was a lump in my throat and, try as I might, I couldn't swallow it.

I got home to find a parcel waiting on the doorstep. Inside it were the first printed copies of my new book, *Casanova's Women*. For any writer, seeing his or her work in print for the first time is both a thrill and a terrifying experience. There's a brief moment of elation: that long slog at your desk has at last become something concrete. But as you open the book, anxiety immediately sets in. You can no longer change a word of what you've written. And since anyone can now read it, you feel vulnerable and exposed.

I picked up one of the books and flicked quickly through the pages, but without much emotion. I had more important things on my mind. So I went downstairs to my study with George at my heels, switched on my computer, and the moment he closed his eyes and went to sleep, Googled the words "mitral" and "valve" and "disease" and "Cavaliers." What I found made for depressing reading. Late onset of MVD in Cavalier King Charles Spaniels often meant that the disease progressed rapidly over the next two years. As well as enlargement of the heart, symptoms could include breathlessness, panting upon exercise, episodic weakness of the hindquarters, flooding of the lungs resulting in pulmonary edema, kidney and liver disorders, and very Victorian-sounding fainting fits.

Oh yes, and weight loss. No danger that we'd reached that point yet.

After I'd read a paragraph that told me

that MVD usually resulted in early death, I shut down the page and went back upstairs. George woke and followed close behind. I served him a healthy lunch of fishy-flavored diet pellets sprinkled with a tiny bit of chopped-up leftover meat, accompanied by a spoonful of the low-fat probiotic yogurt that Kirstie had prescribed a few weeks before to stop him farting. (It worked. Most of the time.) After he'd scoffed the lot, George licked his bowl clean and had a good back scratch on the living room rug. Then he lay down in front of the fridge and stretched out on his side in preparation for his favorite leisure activity: sleeping.

Soon he was snoring loudly and appeared to be out for the count. But one of his eyes remained a fraction open. I saw it following me as I moved from the fridge to the counter and back to the table, preparing a casserole for Joshua's supper. Whenever I went near George, his tail thumped steadily on the ground.

I looked at him, lying there so peacefully, so pleased to have me close to him even when he was half-asleep, and I burst into tears. Because although there was still a slim chance that George might live to the ripe old age of fifteen or sixteen, if he *had* got MVD, as Kirstie suspected, it was far more likely that he'd die within the next two years. And although I was aware that my Cavalier was no spring chicken, two years seemed far too soon for me. Even though he was disobedient, willful, spoiled, and as expensive to run as a Ferrari, I didn't want to lose George. Ever. The idea that I might have to rely on an alarm clock to wake me in the mornings, or that I might read a newspaper all the way through without it getting shredded, or that no one in the house would think that my boring cooking was worthy of three Michelin stars, or that I might come home to find no anxious little face peering out into the darkness through the living room window in the hope of see-ing me — well, frankly none of those things bore thinking about.

I told myself sternly that I was lucky to have had George for so long. After all, I could have lost him on Easter Monday 2005. Police Constable Gary Dodswell, of the Heath Constabulary, who'd come run-ning to George's rescue that day, had brought a case on our behalf against the owners of the Staffordshire bull terrier. He'd not only been shocked by the violence of the attack on George, but also by the severity with which the three or four people who were nominally in charge of the other dog had beaten it even after it had let George go. Prosecuting them under the 1871 Dogs Act, which allowed the police to bring a civil case against the owners of, or people in possession of, a dog dangerously out of control, PC Dodswell had painstakingly gathered evidence, and the case came to court that July. He, Philip, and Sue turned up to give evidence before the magistrates' bench, but the Staffordshire's owners didn't bother to show. They claimed that the monster didn't belong to them, and that they'd only been taking it for a walk. In their absence, the magistrates ruled against them, and an order was issued that their dog should be restrained at all times, and kept muzzled whenever it was in a public place.

It was impossible to know if they'd taken any notice of the ruling. Maybe their stocky canine thug was restrained and muzzled, and maybe he wasn't. Maybe one day George and I would come eyeball to eyeball with him on Hampstead Heath. On PC Dodswell's advice I now kept George on the leash most of the time. Only when I had a clear view of what was coming, and I was pretty certain there were no vicious beasts about, did I dare to let him off it. George was happier that way.

It was beyond me how people could live with vicious dogs. Surely they could train them not to be aggressive. But I guess I was the last person to talk about dog training. As Zach had once noted, it had never been my speciality. Perhaps if I'd stuck to all the rules and tips Janine Grey had given me, George might now have been winning red rosettes for good behavior at dog shows. But I hadn't. Armed with a box of low-cal dog treats, I'd got as far as teaching George to sit and lie down on command — oh yes, and to sleep in the study at night. After that I'd given up.

The thing was, though I was pretty disciplined when it came to my work, where George was concerned I wasn't good at sticking to rules. I was too soft, too indulgent, and, I admit, too lazy. The task of training him required too much time and commitment, and I already spent more than enough time bathing George, walking George, and clearing up the mess of tissues that George had fished out of the waste-paper basket and shredded, not to mention the grass he'd eaten when I wasn't looking, then vomited on my bedroom floor. I was also busy feeding George, grooming George, playing with George, taking George to the dog beauty salon for his bi-monthly hairdo and manicure, tricking George into taking his vitamin pills, and getting George to open his mouth so I could poke around inside it with a baby-size toothbrush and chicken-flavored enzymatic toothpaste so that his remaining teeth didn't fall out. There was a barrier around dog training, and instead of breaking through it with the single-minded commitment of a karate expert kicking through a wall, I'd ambled up to it, nudged at it halfheartedly, then tiptoed away. My excuse was that I didn't want a dog that jumped on command like the von Trapp children in *The Sound of Music.* I liked George as he was — cheeky and mischievous and naughty.

Besides, I told myself at the time, George wasn't really up to a stringent training regime. He was still getting over his injuries. It took him ages to really recover. It wasn't just his nerves; it was also his physical health. During his recuperation he suffered from a bladder infection and a stomach infection. In the autumn, it was a skin infection. He'd always been prone to odd skin ailments, but suddenly they became really bad, and George was scratching himself all the time. He had blackheads and sores all over his belly, itchy bald patches on his legs, and strange scurfy-looking growths on his back. I say strange, because even John, the matter-of-fact veterinary dermatologist we consulted at the end of September, couldn't tell me exactly what they were.

"This could possibly be ringworm," he said as he ran his hands through George's coat in a tail-to-head direction, and peered down at the blotchy skin beneath.

"Ringworm? Ergh!"

He glanced up at me somewhat curiously. "Ringworm isn't actually a worm, you know, it's a fungal infection. Just like athlete's foot." He carried on the examination. "Hmm. On the other hand, this *could* be sarcoptic mange."

"WHAT?" I felt faint.

"Mange," he repeated, pulling off a little crusty scab he'd found, rolling it between his fingers and squinting at it closely. "Otherwise known as scabies. A dog can pick it up from a fox, if it rolls on the grass where a fox has previously been. Are there foxes around where you live?"

"Only on the Heath. Oh yes, and sometimes in our back garden late at night."

"Hmm. That could be it, then. Now mange *is* a parasite. Or rather it's caused by one. *Sarcoptes scabei.* It's a burrowing mite that looks rather like a tiny spider when it's magnified. Wonderful parasite. Mange can cause quite bad hair loss — which would explain these bare patches here on George's back."

"Right." I tried not to go instantly hysterical. "And this mange thing — is it, er, transmittable to humans?"

"Oh yes, it's very contagious. So is ringworm, for that matter."

"Really?"

"It's particularly contagious through direct contact. Like stroking your dog. Or kissing him. Or cuddling him. Any sort of touch, in fact."

Since George was perched on the examination table, I was touching him at that very moment. Even worse, I couldn't let go of him. If I had, he'd have jumped off the table and, given his luck, probably broken all four of his legs.

"And you can pick up both infections indirectly as well," John went on. "From bedding, for instance. Furniture. Carpets. That sort of thing. I don't suppose you ever allow George to jump on the chairs and sofas?"

I nodded. I felt sick. I had visions of athlete's feet sprouting out of my ears and mange mites burrowing through my head. I imagined my hair falling out in clumps when I next washed it. I suddenly began to itch violently all over. I had mange! Soon I'd be bald, covered in scabs, and walking down Hampstead High Street with a hand-bell shouting, "Unclean, unclean!"

"Then again, all these different skin conditions George has could all be caused by a food allergy," John continued. "Or a dust-mite allergy. Or some other allergen. Pollen, perhaps. I'd better test George for those at the same time. As for these blackheads on his belly . . ." He got a piece of sticky tape, pressed it onto the blackheads, and pulled it off. "I'll just go and look at these under the microscope. They're probably crawling with bacteria!" he said cheerfully.

"Um . . . How long will it take to find out what's wrong with George?"

"Ringworm, not so long. Mange — well, the test takes weeks to develop. Sometimes months. I'm afraid there's no rushing the results."

"What will I do until then?" I wailed.

He looked at me as if I was mad. "Carry on as normal, of course! Plus, in the mean-time I'd like you to shampoo George in an antifungal shampoo. Rub it well in. Leave it on for ten minutes. Then rinse off. Don't worry, you don't have to do it every day. Only three times a week."

Poor George! Until the results came

through that Christmas, he was a social outcast. Instead of being clutched to the bosom of every visitor, no one wanted to go near him anymore, not even Joshua or I. As it turned out, his various skin conditions weren't caused by sarcoptic mange *or* ringworm. George was allergic to dozens of domestic allergens which, in turn, made him prone to dozens of bacterial infections. In the spring of 2006 he was successfully treated with expensive antibiotics, anti-inflammatory drugs, and a specially designed immunotherapy vaccine made in the USA and costing yet more hundreds of pounds to import. God bless the pet health insurance company that paid for most of it, including one astronomical bill for £1,016.68 ($2,013.02).

We still hadn't seen the last of George's health troubles. A spiky grass seed burrowed its way deep down into his right ear canal that summer, causing him to shake his head all the time with pain and to scratch his ear until it bled. The vet tried to fish the seed out with a pair of tweezers, but George wouldn't cooperate. In the end she had to give the poor boy a general anesthetic and fish it out when he was asleep.

A fortnight later, Joshua and I took George on holiday to the Cornish coast with our friends the Alwyns and their Jack Russell, Molly. On the very first day, six of us and the dogs scrambled across the rocks for a picnic in an idyllic but inaccessible bay near Prussia Cove. No sooner had we spread out our picnic than there was a terrible yelp: George had found a baited fish hook on the beach and bitten on it. It was protruding from his mouth like a punk's lip ring.

A man on the beach tried to prize the hook out with the aid of his pocket multi-tool (purchased, it turned out, from an Innovations catalog). But the barb was too deeply imbedded in George's flesh, and he was too squeamish to push it through, as were all of us. The picnic was over before it had begun. We packed up our food, clambered back across the rocks, drove miles to a veterinary practice on the edge of an industrial estate, and sat for hours in a gloomy waiting room while poor George was sedated and the fish hook was cut out.

As the vet had said long ago, stuff happened to George.

What with the fish hook, the grass seed, and the twice-weekly immunotherapy injections he needed, it was a good thing that I had so much free time to look after George and Joshua. After Zach and I broke up at Kenwood, I settled down to be what I considered a proper dog owner and mother. To George's horror, I walked him ad infinitum on the Heath. And to Joshua's chagrin, I stayed in every night and cooked him nutritious and, I thought, delicious meals, which were invariably received with the grateful words "Not chicken/chops/spag Bol *again?* Can't I order in a pizza?" Rather than being pleased that his mother was at home so much, offering to test him on his homework or suggesting interesting and improving TV programs that we might watch together, my son seemed slightly miffed. It turned out that, while I'd felt guilty for leaving him home alone when I went out for an evening, he'd liked having the place to himself for a few hours, free of his nagging mama. My Friday and Saturday nights in were a particular disappointment to him because he'd often had his friends around then. They played cards, watched DVDs, listened to loud music, and generally hung out into the early hours, making as much mess and noise as they liked. Now playtime had ended. The killjoy was back in the classroom.

That year I looked at Joshua with an emotion close to amazement. When Udi had died, my son had been a bewildered eight-year-old. Suddenly he was a confident, clever, original young man, poised on the verge of adulthood. Where had the time gone? And what had happened to the stepfather I'd so longed to find for him? He was no longer of an age when he needed or wanted a stepfather in the same way that perhaps he once had. But all was not lost, I realized. Instead of one strong male influence, he'd had several in his life, and each had been valuable to him in his own way. There was Alex, who continued to take him to Arsenal matches, and Philip, who'd always been there for him, and taken him on some unforgettable holidays with Sue and Jessica. There was even Joshua's old archenemy, Anthony. Now that he and I were just friends, he and Joshua had become big buddies, and Anthony teased him good-naturedly about what a pest he used to be. There was also someone else who'd become an influence on Joshua: our wonderful new next-door neighbor. Since he'd lost his own father when he was young, this kind person knew what it was like for a boy not to have a man around to steer him into the right career, and he'd generously offered to take Joshua under his professional wing and give him a taste of the financial world that my business-minded son was determined to be part of one day.

Nearly a year following our breakup, Zach was also on the scene again. Though in many ways both our lives had been much easier when we were apart, we'd found that we'd missed each other. So when we finally got back together, we swore that this time we'd do our best to make sure that we stayed that way. I tried not to expect more on the domestic front than he could reasonably offer me, and in return Zach came up to Hampstead more often, ganged up with Joshua against me, and occasionally even took George for his late-night walk. I can't say that he looked at ease, marching down the street in his immaculate trench coat with our giant pom-pom trotting alongside him. His head was lowered in case someone he knew saw him, and he held the leash at arm's length, as if he were convinced it would give him bubonic plague. As for poop-scooping — well, some things are too much to ask of anyone.

Zach was still a long way from becoming a dog lover or a family man, but I lived in hope. Miracles happened. You never knew what life was going to throw at you. One minute you were walking along the road, head held high, smug and invincible. The next you were flat on your face on the tarmac, cut, bruised, and convinced you'd never stand up again. It took time to get over the emotional and physical bruising, but eventually you did. Something lifted you out of your misery, and you discovered you were happy again.

As my father used to say, "The happiest people in the world are those with the lowest expectations." I think he meant that happiness lay in appreciating what you had, rather than yearning for what you hadn't. And if I'd learned anything through losing Dad and Udi in such close proximity, it was to enjoy the small things in life.

Such as sharing a private joke with my sister and mother.

And talking later into the night with Tabby and Hannah.

And taking George for a walk on a cold winter's morning, when the grass on the Heath was so thick with frost that it looked as if it were embroidered with sequins.

And, above all, hearing Joshua's laughter, as he lounged on the sofa doing his homework while simultaneously watching a football match on television, playing a card game on his laptop, eating a pizza, and texting a friend on his mobile phone.

In other words, multitasking, just like his father used to.

AFTERWORD

Long ago I told Joshua that surviving Udi's death would be tough, but we'd manage it somehow. I look at my son now — so grown-up, so confident, so much his own person — and I know that, somewhat miraculously, we have.

I suppose we could have done it without our dog, but it would have been much harder.

As I write, George continues to dominate our day-to-day existence. He's been our loyal friend and companion for the last eight and a half years, and has seen Joshua and me through our darkest days. The moment he crossed our threshold, the word *home* had a warm ring to it, the ring it had lost on the terrible day when the one and only Udi Eichler walked out of his front door for the very last time, leaving behind him a future he would never experience, and a son he wouldn't live to see grow up.

George found us when we were lost, and anchored us when we were adrift. He's warmed our hearts, kept us on our toes, and often reduced us to hysterical laughter, all without saying a word. He's kept us awake for countless nights, seen off one of my boyfriends, and at times driven us barking mad. Still, Joshua and I wouldn't be without him for anything. The proof of it is that he's got me out for a walk practically every single morning, even in the pouring rain — greater love hath no woman, particularly when she's just washed and blow-dried her hair.

George is now approaching sixty in dog years and, sadly, he's beginning to show his age. And the older he gets, the more high-maintenance he becomes. To date, he's cost around £15,000 ($30,000) in vet's bills, dog hotel bills, hairdos, dog food, and pet insurance, and the amount of time I've spent looking after him is incalculable. But, tell me, what are time and money for, other than spending on the people and things you love?

We're off to see some veterinary cardiologists next week so that George can have a heart scan. No doubt they'll recommend medication, angioplasty, or even open-heart surgery. Not to mention a month's recuperation at some expensive canine spa. It's hard to come to terms with the fact that there's something really wrong with George, because he still looks very healthy. Perhaps that's because he's on the chunky side. Or fat, as Joshua puts it. Or huge, as Sue says more bluntly. Like most of the country, our dog's on a permanent diet, and like most of the country he doesn't stick to it. And whose fault is that? you may well ask.

But no matter what adjective you use to describe George's girth, to us he's still as handsome as he was on the day we first saw him running up Mrs. Colman's stairs. Call me shallow if you like, but I never stop appreciating how beautiful he is. When he's curled up asleep by the open fire, for instance, with his freckled nose resting between his big paws and the tip of his tongue protruding from his lips like a little pink postage stamp. Or when he comes hurtling toward me across a field, with his long ears flapping in the wind. Or when he's stalking a squirrel in the woods and, poised to chase it, stands with one front paw raised like the hunting dog he's descended from. On occasions such as these, my podgy pooch still manages to look gorgeous, aristocratic, even delicate, and I can't help going gooey inside when I look at him.

As for the inner dog, George is still as

sweet and adorable and loyal as ever. No man has ever loved me as unconditionally as he does, and I'm quite certain that no man ever will. He's tolerant to the point of being passive, and restful to the point of being comatose. But he's stubborn, too. He still hasn't realized that "no" means "no," or that balls are for chasing, and he can't understand the "fetch" command, so perhaps he's not the brainiest dog in the world. Or maybe the opposite is true. For a creature who speaks no language known to humans, George certainly knows how to get what he wants from them: a walk, a cuddle, attention, food.

Thankfully, I've managed to establish a little authority over George during the past year. I've even managed to teach the old dog one or two new tricks. Lying down to command, for instance. And, more important, spending the night alone. Actually, I think he likes that more than I do. On nights when Zach's not around, I sometimes sneak into the study, pick George up, carry him down the hall, and plonk him on the end of my duvet. He lies there for a while, quietly keeping me company, but he eventually slips off the bed, plods back into his own room, and curls up in his comfortable, fake-fur nest. He, too, is beginning to relish his independence.

Hold on — I can hear barking up in the kitchen. Now it's stopped. Now it's started again. Now it's stopped. Here comes the pitter-patter of paw steps, tumbling down the stairs. George pushes open my study door with his black button nose, marches in, comes straight up to me, and places his hairy front paws firmly on my knees. He arches his back in a big stretch, then inches forward with little dancing steps.

"Hello, Georgie-Porgie!" I bend down to kiss the white downy fluff that grows upright on top of his head.

Georgie-Porgie smiles up at me lovingly. I smile back. His dark eyes stare meaningfully into mine. Oh dear. Something tells me this isn't just a social call.

George licks his lips. I look at my watch. It's five o'clock, his suppertime.

"You'll have to wait," I tell him, as I push his paws off my lap. "I'm still working."

George doesn't buy it. He wants his food, and he wants it now. His smile changes to a determined expression. He leaps onto the daybed next to me and, in order to get as near to me as possible, perches on the edge, like a parrot, with his claws hanging over the side. I can feel his eyes boring into my head. When I don't turn and look at him, he starts to whine quietly.

I remember what Janine Grey taught me, and I take no notice. I will not reward attention-seeking behavior. It's time he learned who's top dog around here! But even though I ignore him, George's whines become louder, more insistent, more annoying until . . .

Excuse me, but I have to go. The King of the Canines has called.

ABOUT THE AUTHOR

Judith Summers is the author of eight books, including *Casanova's Women: The Great Seducer and the Women He Loved.* She lives in London with her son, Joshua, and the ever-entertaining George.

We hope you have enjoyed this Large Print book. Other Thorndike, Wheeler, and Chivers Press Large Print books are available at your library or directly from the publishers.

For information about current and upcoming titles, please call or write, without obligation, to:

Publisher
Thorndike Press
295 Kennedy Memorial Drive
Waterville, ME 04901
Tel. (800) 223-1244

or visit our Web site at:

http://gale.cengage.com/thorndike

OR

Chivers Large Print
published by BBC Audiobooks Ltd
St James House, The Square
Lower Bristol Road
Bath BA2 3SB
England
Tel. +44(0) 800 136919
email: bbcaudiobooks@bbc.co.uk
www.bbcaudiobooks.co.uk

All our Large Print titles are designed for easy reading, and all our books are made to last.